D1233758

CROSSCURRENTS *Modern Critiques*
Harry T. Moore, *General Editor*

Richard D. Lehan

F. Scott Fitzgerald
AND THE CRAFT OF FICTION

WITH A PREFACE BY
Harry T. Moore

Carbondale and Edwardsville

SOUTHERN ILLINOIS UNIVERSITY PRESS

FEFFER AND SIMONS, INC.

London and Amsterdam

For Ann

The quotations from various works of F. Scott Fitzgerald
that appear in this book are protected by copyright and have
been reprinted here by special permission of
Charles Scribner's Sons.

Quotations from the *Crack-Up*, ed. Edmund Wilson,
copyright 1945 by New Directions,
are reprinted by permission of the publisher,
New Directions Publishing Corporation.

FIRST PUBLISHED, OCTOBER 1966
SECOND PRINTING, MAY 1967

Copyright © 1966 by Southern Illinois University Press
All rights reserved
Library of Congress Catalog Card Number 66–15059
Printed in the United States of America
Designed by Andor Braun

PREFACE

RICHARD D. LEHAN *begins his excellent book on F. Scott Fitzgerald by saying that the fictional writing of this author has* "received as much attention as that of any American novelist, with the exception of perhaps Melville, James, Hemingway and Faulkner." *Some of us can remember when Fitzgerald was neglected—Melville, too, for that matter, as well as James and even Faulkner. Hemingway seems always to have been the lucky boy, and of all these writers he least deserves to be in this group; he had a talent, but a comparatively limited one.*

Melville's greatness was first appreciated in the 1920s. Lewis Mumford's book on him in 1929 was most instrumental in bringing him to public attention; Mumford plausibly demonstrated that Melville was not only a great author of America but of the world. He had suffered nearly a century of neglect. As for James, he was never really popular; the short novel Daisy Miller (1879) was his nearest approach to a success in the marketplace. By the time James died in 1916 everyone was speaking of him as an author's author, difficult if not impossible to read. His rise to prominence on reading lists began after his centennial in 1943, when the Kenyon Review brought out a James issue. By the end of the Second World War, the James revival was going strongly.

And at that time the Faulkner revival began. Faulk-

ner had rarely found a wide public except for Sanctuary (1931), which he later said he had written in a sensational manner in order to make some money. When Malcolm Cowley, at the end of the Second World War, was assembling material for The Portable Faulkner, he found that all of Faulkner's books were out of print. Cowley's wide-ranging selection from them brought Faulkner to public attention, and eventually he became a best seller and Nobel Prize winner, although he had long since exhausted his talent. Meanwhile, Hemingway had been going strong, a legend as well as a writer, though his own finest work was behind him: his early short stories and his first two genuine novels, The Sun Also Rises (1926) and A Farewell to Arms (1929).

Fitzgerald in his early youth had the bad luck to score an immediate success with his first novel, This Side of Paradise (1920). He and his wife Zelda were golden and glamorous, and they couldn't stand the pace of success. In order to live high, Fitzgerald cruelly drove himself to write Saturday Evening Post stories with an artificial glitter. His serious novel, The Great Gatsby (1925), was a critical success, but it didn't sell on the grand scale. In a few years he found himself with a psychotic wife, a fading reputation, and a fierce ambition to write a great novel—while still trying to meet expenses through depressing hackwork. He felt that in Tender Is the Night (1934) he had written a great book. He had, but the public didn't take it up. The rest of his life, until his premature death at forty-four in 1940, is a true horror story, best told in Arthur Mizener's biography, The Far Side of Paradise (1951; revised edition 1965). Fitzgerald toward the end rallied his forces and made one final desperate attempt with The Last Tycoon. He didn't live to finish it, but the parts of the book that exist reveal that it deserves to be considered on a level with Gatsby and Tender.

In the present study Mr. Lehan searches for Fitzgerald's roots in the Romantic movement. He traces

Fitzgerald's inspiration to Keats, which has been done before, but Mr. Lehan further shows that Fitzgerald was also influenced by decadents of the late-nineteenth-century phase of the Romantic movement, such as Ernest Dowson and Walter Pater. Mr. Lehan's book is full of rewarding insights, and if he has to go over some already familiar territory, two points may be made about that. One, Mr. Lehan owes this to newcomers to the Fitzgerald reading experience, who have not been through such expert books as, say, Henry Dan Piper's F. Scott Fitzgerald: A Critical Portrait (1965). Two, Mr. Lehan works the material brilliantly, and to what has already been known and said he adds a great deal in the way of a fresh approach. Seasoned readers of Fitzgerald will find that Mr. Lehan will deepen their own understanding of Fitzgerald's work.

Mr. Lehan is particularly good at getting at the essential problems of Jay Gatsby and of Dr. Dick Diver of Tender Is the Night. This critic sees the origin of Gatsby's tragedy in the intensity of his dream, Diver's in being "sidetracked by the very rich and by his own weakness, which was to feel needed and be the center of attention." He notes that "whereas The Great Gatsby was a novel about what could never be, Tender Is the Night is a novel about what could have been. . . . Both Gatsby and Dick Diver believed that they could make time stand still; Gatsby thought he could recapture the lost past, and Dick Diver thought that his future would wait for him. Fitzgerald suggests that both were not aware of the nature of time." Keats, in "Ode to a Nightingale" (which gave Tender Is the Night its title) longed "for a state of eternality while recognizing that he [was] subject to a state of temporality." But Keats and Fitzgerald "knew that no such world was possible for men," something Jay Gatsby never learned and Dick Diver learned too late.

In dealing with such matters, Mr. Lehan is very good; and he explores every phase of Fitzgerald rewardingly. He sometimes helpfully uses background material—he casts new light, for example, on Fitzgerald's early relationship with the Chicago North Shore heiress, Ginevra King, who with her family left a particular stamp upon his work. Indeed, Mr. Lehan throughout makes acute observations about the people Fitzgerald knew and their importance to his work—for, as Mr. Lehan several times points out, Fitzgerald wrote best when he was drawing directly on his own experience.

Mr. Lehan correctly assesses the weaknesses of Tender Is the Night, though he doesn't make the usual objections to the "Rosemary beginning"—with the opening section of the book on the Riviera. As most readers know, Fitzgerald in his puzzlement over the novel's failure to achieve an immediate success, said he should have put first what he originally presented as the second part of the story, and he cut up and rearranged a copy of the book to conform with this idea, placing the Rosemary section after the part which had followed it as a flashback. This version of the novel was published after his death, but current editions go back to Fitzgerald's original order, apparently because so many teachers who use the novel in their courses prefer the Rosemary beginning, for which Mr. Lehan makes out a good case.

As indicated above, Mr. Lehan is right in diagnosing the weaknesses of Tender; but the book is sufficiently powerful, I think, to rise above them. It is certainly Fitzgerald's masterpiece. Beside it, Gatsby is a tour de force, an immensely good one, but with air of contrivance. And Gatsby himself is not really tragic in the great, noble, classical sense; he is no more than a pathetic figure. On the other hand, Dick Diver is genuinely tragic.

First of all, in the classic pattern, he falls from high place—not just socially, but spiritually. He is a man of distinction, a skilled scientist, an accomplished healer. And he is a successful theoretician of his craft, the author of a small book recognized as important in the area of psychiatry. He is indeed no ordinary hero, but almost super-human in his abilities. Nevertheless he has the human frailties which make him not too good nor yet too bad, as a man; since he doesn't, then, have either the remoteness of a saint or a villain, he can attract our sympathy. As few modern fictional characters do, Dick Diver fulfills the requirements for the classical tragic hero. He qualifies further in that he is self-destroyed. Jay Gatsby, for all his pathos, is insignificant beside Dr. Diver.

Similarly, other parts of Tender Is the Night are on the grand scale, despite Fitzgerald's uncertainties about it and despite those limitations in the Post stories. Fitzgerald's language is here seen and felt at its finest in the richly toned descriptions of the Riviera, of Rome, and of Zürich and the Lake of Zug region, as well as in its vital accounts of action and its precisely right conversations.

The symbolic references—from "the bright tan prayer rug of a beach" (where we watch the people whose playing is their praying) to Dick Diver's last unsteady attempt to make a sign of benediction above his former "parish"—are highly effective, like the valley of ashes in The Great Gatsby. In Tender we have an extremely convincing set of characters, some of them (as Mr. Lehan points out) interestingly parallel. The story itself, apart from the "theme," has a fascination that keeps readers going as apparently it didn't in proletarian-conscious 1934; and the "theme," which as Mr. Lehan also indicates resembles that of Gatsby, is expertly worked out. With Tender we have a deep and complicated book that is an important commentary on modern life, and it is reassuring to see it finding a place in the literature of our time.

Richard D. Lehan helps to place the book, as well as Fitzgerald's other significant work, in this context. He also does something which has been too rarely attempted with Fitzgerald: he finds him a distinct place in the American writing and discusses him in terms of such writers as Thoreau, James, and Hawthorne. It can safely be said, now, that Fitzgerald is at last receiving the recognition he deserves, with the fine biography by Arthur Mizener, the commentary of Lionel Trilling, the revealing textual study of Tender by Matthew J. Bruccoli, and the critical volumes of Henry Dan Piper and Sergio Perosa; and with the present book. Last, not least, among these works, Richard D. Lehan's is an impressive achievement, both in the area of Fitzgerald studies and in that of modern criticism itself.

HARRY T. MOORE

Southern Illinois University
March 4, 1966

CONTENTS

INTRODUCTION

THE FICTION of F. Scott Fitzgerald has received as much attention as that of any American novelist, with the exception perhaps of Melville, James, Hemingway and Faulkner. If we consider the plight of Fitzgerald when he died on December 21, 1940, we can find an all too pathetic irony in this. If we consider the achievement of the man—an achievement in the face of the cruelest difficulties—we can also find a satisfying justice.

The story of Fitzgerald the man has been told often and told well, and the commentaries on his fiction help us to see the complexity of his best work. This book, attempting to reconcile both biography and criticism, is concerned with the quality of Fitzgerald's developing imagination. I have tried to place Fitzgerald within the traditions of nineteenth- and twentieth-century literature, showing the Romantic quality of his imagination and illustrating the similarities of themes between Fitzgerald and Keats, Swinburne, Pater, Dowson, Rupert Brooke, Oscar Wilde, Frank Norris, H. G. Wells, Joseph Conrad, as well as Oswald Spengler whose influence on Fitzgerald has been surprisingly overlooked. I have also tried to analyze the themes and meaning of Fitzgerald's fiction in terms of the experiences from which they were drawn, to show the changing attitude that Fitzgerald took toward this experience, to describe the emotional disposition he brought to each novel, and to show how he learned to control and sustain that emotion with a developing sense of craft. I have considered the relationships between Fitzgerald and his most important contemporaries—Ernest Hemingway and William Faulkner—and examined and assessed Fitzgerald's literary reputation today, indicating what he was best able to do and what he was unable to do as a novelist, perhaps because limitations in his own emotional makeup and experience affected the way he handled his material.

When Fitzgerald was writing well, he was writing out of a deeply personal sense of experience. Fitzgerald's fiction is at times an exercise in self-pity and self-justification, and he often used the novel to settle old scores—to excoriate in his imagination people who had hurt him in life. His main themes—the theme of youth, success, and money—stem from attitudes founded on personal experiences—experiences often romantically removed to a heightened world. In time Fitzgerald learned to control this heightened sense of life, to find ways to objectify his emotions, and to establish an ironic distance. Fitzgerald had a kind of incremental imagination, and he first worked his ideas into his stories and later into the novels, deepening and enriching the texture as he moved from story to novel. Thus the critical tendency to emphasize the mythic nature of Fitzgerald's characters—especially Gatsby—is misleading because although Gatsby does embody something in the American experience, he embodies something first in Fitzgerald's own experience—something on the personal level that is far different from what it means on the symbolic or mythic level. The fact that Fitzgerald wrote so directly from his own sense of experience is, as I shall try to show, both the source of his strength and the source of his weakness as a novelist.

In writing this book I have incurred a number of obligations. I am most grateful to Mrs. Ginevra King

Pirie and her sister, Mrs. Marjorie King Belden, who knew Fitzgerald at a crucial moment in his life, and who generously shared their memories and impressions with me. I am deeply grateful to Dr. and Mrs. Richard D. Evans for arranging a number of interviews for me and for many other kindnesses. I should like to thank Alexander Clark, Curator of Special Collections in the Firestone Library at Princeton University, who put the Fitzgerald papers and manuscripts at my disposal—also Edward Everett Horton, Budd Schulberg, Ralph Ellison, Mrs. Frances Kroll Ring, and Robert Mulligan (of Pakula and Mulligan Productions) who answered my queries or assisted me in other ways. And I am particularly grateful to Professors Blake Nevius, John Espey, Frederick J. Hoffman, and Harry T. Moore for reading the manuscript and making many useful suggestions, and to Mrs. Marilyn Hails for her conscientious and thorough job of editing.

My supreme debt here, as over the past ten years, is to Fred Hoffman, who has been a constant source of encouragement and help as well as a model of scholarly dedication and professional integrity.

RICHARD D. LEHAN

University of California, Los Angeles
November 1, 1965

F. Scott Fitzgerald
AND THE CRAFT OF FICTION

F. SCOTT FITZGERALD
AND THE ROMANTIC
TRADITION

> *Golden lads and girls all must*
> *Like chimney-sweepers come to dust.*

"Now, no romantic would have written that," said T. E. Hulme of these lines from Shakespeare's *Cymbeline*. "He would have to write golden youth, and take up the thing at least a couple of notes in pitch."[1]

While Hulme did not have F. Scott Fitzgerald in mind, his words well describe the quality of Fitzgerald's imagination. If (as Hulme suggests) Romanticism involves a heightened view of reality, if (as Alex Comfort remarks) it "is a force which alone among artistic forces seems to preserve perpetual virility and perpetual youth,"[2] if (as Herbert Read insists) it is an artistic perspective which makes "men more conscious of the terror and the beauty, the *wonder* of the possible forms of being,"[3] and, finally, if "Romanticism is the endeavor . . . to achieve . . . [the] illusioned view . . . of human life which is produced by an imaginative fusion of the familiar and the strange, the known and the unknown, the real and the ideal,"[4] then F. Sott Fitzgerald is a Romantic. For Fitzgerald idealized youth, that splendid moment of imaginative commitment with its sense of wonder and its trusts in life's boundless possibility and opportunity.

According to Morse Peckham, the Romantics believed that the universe was alive and that fulfillment was a process of growth. Such a process of becoming led to a continued sense of expectation.[5] Fitzgerald never had so sophisticated a view as this—the Romantics themselves probably never did—but Peckham gives us a brilliant philosophical explanation of the assumptions, in many cases unexamined assumptions, behind the Romantic attitude, and they are assumptions shared by Fitzgerald's characters:

[Amory Blaine, of *This Side of Paradise*] wondered how people could fail to notice that he was a boy marked for glory.[6]

[Anthony Patch, of *The Beautiful and Damned*] thrilled to remote harmonies . . . for he was young now as he would never be again, and more triumphant than death.[7]

[Gatsby had] some heightened sensitivity to the promises of life . . . an extraordinary gift for hope, a romantic readiness.[8]

In the spring of 1917, when Doctor Richard Diver [of *Tender Is the Night*] first arrived in Zurich, he was twenty-six years old, a fine age for a man, indeed, the very acme of bachelorhood . . . [bringing with him] the illusions of eternal strength and health, and of the essential goodness of people; illusions of a nation.[9]

[Monroe Stahr, of *The Last Tycoon*] had flown up very high to see, on strong wings, when he was young. And while he was up there he had looked on all the kingdoms, with the kind of eyes that can stare straight into the sun.[10]

The last metaphor—the metaphor of flight—is especially appropriate to suggest the spirit of adventure, the sense of yearning, that characterizes the Romantic hero. As Hulme has noticed, for such an individual life "is an infinite reservoir of possibilites," and this "attitude seems to crystallize . . . round metaphors of flight. Hugo is always flying, flying over abysses, flying up into the eternal gases." [11]

The flight suggests a desire for experience and a quest for meaning and the attainment of beauty. In "The Everlasting Yea" Carlyle described this feeling as an almost religious commitment to life. When this attitude of mind leads to desires that are impossible to achieve, it becomes destructive and self-defeating. Keats's lovers—Lamia, Endymion, Hyperion—are often destroyed this way, and so is Jay Gatsby and, in another sense, Monroe Stahr.

If the hero is not physically destroyed by such disillusionment, his life suddenly loses its purpose; it becomes absurd; and the hero becomes the eternal wanderer, alienated from society, an outcast and a scapegoat. In "The Everlasting No" Carlyle described this as a kind of despair that comes with the loss of commitment. Such is the despair of Byron's Harold, Manfred, and Cain, and of Shelley's Alastor. Such also is the attitude of Amory Blaine (whom Fitzgerald described as a Childe Harold) [12] and of Dick Diver. Anthony Patch moves back and forth between these two states of mind—between the Everlasting Yea and the Everlasting No—committing himself when it is too late, when he has already been beaten by time.

Time is the real enemy in the Romantic world. Man is subject to mutability; "youth grows pale, and specter-thin, and dies." "There is a space of life between boyhood and maturity [wrote Keats] in which the soul is in a ferment, the characters undecided, the way of life uncertain, the ambition thick-sighted." [13] This is the moment of youthful commitment. When it is wasted it brings on Romantic sadness; when it is remembered it brings on Romantic nostalgia.

Fitzgerald experienced these emotions, and he portrayed them in personal terms in his novels. He at the same time was aware of how these matters had been handled in the history of literature, and no one has yet demonstrated Fitzgerald's knowledge and use of the Romantic tradition.

The tradition has its beginning with Jean-Jacques Rousseau, a writer that Fitzgerald read with interest.[14]

The Confessions sets the pattern for the Romantic journey. Rousseau seems continually discontented with his lot, and his sense of adventure is coupled with a yearning for something better. He idealizes experience—especially his love for Louise de Warens—and he is disappointed and disillusioned when the reality of that love falls beneath his sense of imaginative expectation. Rousseau lives in a world of imagination; sometimes, as he puts it himself, so he can forget his real condition.[15] His dreams lead inevitably to disillusionment; his sense of hope gives way ultimately to a state of loss. Rousseau's state of mind upon losing Louise is very similar to Gatsby's feelings (expressed by Nick Carraway) upon losing Daisy.

> [Gatsby] must have felt that he had lost the old warm world, paid a high price for living too long with a single dream [says Nick]. He must have looked up at an unfamiliar sky through frightening leaves and shivered as he found what a grotesque thing a rose is. [162]

> All the sweet dreams I had indulged with such affection disappeared [writes Rousseau]. . . . It was a frightful moment; and those that followed it were just as dark. I was still young, but that pleasant feeling of joy and hope that enlivens youth left me for ever. [249]

Byron called Rousseau "the apostle of affliction,"[16] and believed that Rousseau was "kindled" and then "blasted" by the overweening desire to realize an "ideal beauty"—a desire which Byron called "a foolish quest." This is, of course, the chastened Byron speaking, the man who has been "weaned" of "the weary dream." Fitzgerald compared Amory Blaine to Childe Harold, and *This Side of Paradise* ends on the same note that Byron begins Canto III of *Childe Harold*. In both works, the hero admits that his experiences have brought disillusionment. "My springs of life were poisoned," says Byron, speaking for both himself and Childe Harold. Fitzgerald, picking up the same metaphor, says that "the waters of disillusion had left a deposit on [Amory's] soul" [282]. Both Amory and Harold, like Manfred, want a chance to forget in order to recoup their powers—Byron describing a "Forgetfulness around me," and Amory a "time and the absence of ulterior pressure" [281]. Although the tone is essentially pessimistic, both Amory and Harold feel that they can rise again, on surer wings, out of the ashes of the past. They both speak of the need to overcome their "selfishness." Byron, again speaking of himself, insists that he has the "strength to bear what time cannot abate." Harold also has a newfound sense of maturity.

> Harold, once more within the vortex roll'd
> On with giddy circle, chasing Time
> Yet within a nobler aim than in his youth's
>   fond [foolish] prime. [III, 11 Woods,
>   p. 550]

Amory, too, is confident that he "can bring poise and balance into [his] life." Amory was "not sorry for himself—art, politics, religion, whatever his medium should be, he knew was safe now, free from all hysteria—he could accept what was acceptable, roam, grow, rebel, sleep deep . . . [282]. *This Side of Paradise* and *Childe Harold* thus share a state of mind, and both are studies in the process and effect of youthful disillusionment.

Although the first paragraph of *This Side of Paradise* opens with reference to Byron, the Romantic poet who had the most influence on Fitzgerald was not Byron but John Keats. Fitzgerald idealized Keats, the poet who so brilliantly depicted the transitory nature of beauty and whose hopeless love for Fanny Brawne was cut off, like his poetry, in the very bud of youth. Fitzgerald wrote his daughter in the summer of 1940:

"The Grecian Urn" is unbearably beautiful with every syllable as inevitable as the notes in Beethoven's Ninth Symphony. . . . I suppose I've read it a hundred times.

About the tenth time I began to know what it was about, and caught the chime in it and the exquisite inner mechanics. Likewise with "The Nightingale" which I can never read through without tears in my eyes; likewise the "Pot of Basil" ["Isabella"] with its great stanzas about the two brothers, "Why were they proud, etc."; and "The Eve of St. Agnes," which has the richest, most sensuous imagery in English, not excepting Shakespeare. And finally his three or four great sonnets, "Bright Star" and the others.[17]

And in a letter to James Boyd, five years earlier, Fitzgerald comments on the similarity of their writing —that they share "a sort of nostalgic sadness" which is perhaps "because we both read Keats a lot when we were young." [18]

There is no doubt that Keats was one of the most important influences, both in theme and style, on Fitzgerald's writing, and that Keats's presence can be seen and felt throughout Fitzgerald's fiction. In *This Side of Paradise*, Amory read "the 'Belle Dame Sans Merci'; [and] for a month was keen on naught else" [51]. And Amory, with Tom D'Invillers, recited "The Ode to a Nightingale," and then felt depressed because he knew that he would never be able to write such beautiful poetry. " 'I don't catch the subtle things like "silver-snarling trumpets" [he says]. I may turn out an intellectual, but I'll never write anything but mediocre poetry' " [84].

The Fitzgerald novel which most shows the Keatsian influence is *The Beautiful and Damned*. Fitzgerald originally intended to call it *The Beautiful Lady Without Mercy* after Keats's "La Belle Dame Sans Merci," and there is a scene in the novel where a world-weary knight enters a monastery and is lured to his death at the sight of a beautiful girl passing under his window. Although Anthony tells this story tongue-in-cheek, it is strangely an appropriate tale for him because he also suffers from world-weariness; becomes a kind of dandy, contemptuous of his more ambitious riends; and is eventually defeated by "time" when he makes the pursuit of youth and beauty (personified by Gloria) an end in itself. "She was a sun, radiant, growing, gathering light and storing it—then . . . pouring it forth in a glance . . . to that part of him that cherished all beauty and all illusion" [73]. Anthony is damned (as the title suggests) by his desire to attain an immutable beauty. This theme immediately brings to mind "Ode on a Grecian Urn" and "Ode to a Nightingale." Like the lovers on the urn, Anthony feels "young now . . . and more triumphant than death" [126]. In his ode, Keats told us that melancholy "dwells with Beauty—Beauty that must die." Like Wallace Stevens, Keats felt that death was the mother of beauty, and what was beautiful became poignant as it wasted in the vault of time. Anthony and Gloria share this sentiment. " 'There's no beauty without poignancy [says Gloria] and there's no poignancy without the feeling that it's going, men, names, books, houses—bound for dust—mortal' " [167]. " 'Even Gloria's beauty needed wild emotions, needed poignancy, needed death,' " says Anthony later on, repeating Gloria's words.

In the "Ode on a Grecian Urn," Keats maintains that beauty and truth exist in the realm of art, beyond time. In both "Ode to a Nightingale" and "Ode on Melancholy" he tells us that wine can help us escape the pain of lost youth.

> O for a draught of vintage! . . .
> That I might drink, and leave the world unseen,
> And with thee [the nightingale] fade away
>   into the forest dim:
> Fade far away, and quite forget . . .
> The weariness, the fever, and the fret . . .
> Where youth grows pale, and spectre-thin,
>   and dies. [Woods, p. 857]

Fitzgerald made specific use of both these ideas in *The Beautiful and Damned,* and as Anthony grows older, we are told—in obvious Keatsian imagery and language—that after "those things [of beauty faded] . . . there was wine":

> The fruit of youth or of the grape, the transitory magic of the brief passage from darkness to darkness—the old illusion that truth and beauty were in some way entwined. [417]

Anthony and Gloria live in a world of illusions that Lamia builds for her lover, the world of ideals that the Moon erected for Endymion, the world of order ruled over by Hyperion, the realm beyond time symbolized by Keats's nightingale, Grecian urn, and Baiae's isle. The lovers on the urn are "forever panting, and forever young." At the end of *The Beautiful and Damned*, Anthony, a wreck of a man, longs for Italy and "the romance of the blue canals in Venice, of the golden green hills of Fiesole after rain, and of women . . . *who were always beautiful and always young*" [444, italics mine.]. Quite literally Anthony longs to be a part of that "foster-child of silence and slow time." He and Gloria realize that the moment gives beauty its meaning, and yet they desire to live as if they were beyond time, like the eternal lovers on the urn. This is the Romantic flight from reality, the desire for a world beyond time, an ideal world where the laws of nature do not apply.

Keats's influence on *The Great Gatsby* is more remote, although Tristram Coffin attempted to establish a parallel between this novel and "La Belle Dame Sans Merci" as well as to the *Märchen* tale, typed by Aarne and Thompson as Mt. 561, the pattern of which Coffin describes as follows:

I] The hero finds a magic object which will perform all the wishes of the owner.

II] By means of the object he builds a magic castle and marries the king's daughter.

III] The magic object is stolen by a third person who

wants to possess the wife. The castle and the wife are transported to a distant island.

v] The hero recovers the object with the help of a second magic object which transports the hero to the island. The castle and the princess are restored.[19]

Except for Section IV, this does parallel the pattern of *The Great Gatsby*, but it does not really tell us very much about the meaning of the novel or the quality of Fitzgerald's imagination, because, as Coffin willingly admits, "no scholar would be bold enough to claim that Fitzgerald consciously conceived of Gatsby's dream in terms of a formal *Märchen*." One could make an equally good case for a parallel between *The Great Gatsby* and *Troilus and Cressida*, with Nick Carraway fulfilling the role of Pander. The point is that once the novel is reduced to a skeleton design, one has destroyed the imaginative conception behind it—the way the artistic mind was influenced and was working at the time of creation—and all kinds of irrelevant connections can be made. This is not to say that Keats was not in Fitzgerald's mind when he was writing *The Great Gatsby*. During Nick's first visit to the Buchanans, Daisy remarks:

> "I looked outdoors for a minute, and its very romantic outdoors. There's a bird on the lawn that I think must be a nightingale come over on the Cunard or White Star Line. He's singing away. . . . It's romantic, isn't it, Tom?" [16]

For Tom, the materialist, incapable of comprehending the metaphorical and symbolic meaning of the nightingale—this bird that "was not born for death" —it is not romantic at all, and he changes the conversation immediately to talk about the stable. Here Fitzgerald relies upon an understanding of Keats to reveal aspects of character that are important to the meaning of the novel.

If Gatsby tries to approximate the flight of the

nightingale, Anthony Patch and Dick Diver ar
"tolled back" to their "sole self." The title *Tender I
the Night* is, of course, taken from "Ode to a Night
ingale," and Fitzgerald prefaces his novel with ;
quotation from the poem.

> *Already with thee! tender is the night* . . .
> . . . *But here there is no light,*
> *Save what from heaven is with breezes blown*
> *Through verdurous glooms and winding mossy ways.*

There has recently been an attempt to see a point b
point parallelism between the structure of *Tender I
the Night* and "Ode to a Nightingale." [20] This pushe
the case too far and fails to give Fitzgerald's imagina
tion its proper latitude. A more convincing case can b
made by comparing the tone of the two works, fo
they have much in common—especially the melan
choly effect of time on the vitality of youth, the wa
sense of world weariness, and the rueful desire fo
"easeful death." Both works brilliantly suggest a mo
ment of time grown overripe and anticipate th
sadness of beauty's decay; both evoke a sense o
gloomy night—a world where "there is no light," a
Keats puts it, or where one feels "alone with eacl
other in the dark universe," as Fitzgerald says. Rose
mary Hoyt, the spirit of youth and beauty, seems a
immortal as the nightingale—especially to Dick Dive
—and when Abe North comes upon her, alone and
pensive late at night, he makes the connection be
tween Rosemary and the spirit of the nightingale:

> "Plagued by the nightingale," Abe suggested, and
> repeated, "probably plagued by the nightingale." [42]

Although the influence of Keats is more difficult to
detect in *The Last Tycoon,* we know from Sheilah
Graham that Keats was still his favorite poet. He
could recite by heart "Ode on a Grecian Urn," and he
excited Miss Graham into reading both Byron's col
lected works and the poetry of Keats, insisting on the

910 Oxford edition: *The Poetical Works of John Keats,* and editing his own version of "La Belle Dame ans Merci" because he disliked Leigh Hunt's edi-on.[21]

No other poet probably had a more lasting effect on itzgerald than Keats. Yet he read many poets—espe-ially when he was at Princeton—and when he began riting *This Side of Paradise* he was deeply immersed post-Romantic as well as Romantic poetry. Henry)an Piper has described the literary environment at rinceton when Fitzgerald was there.[22] The decadent r esthetic movement dominated the undergraduate terest, and everyone was reading Swinburne, Pater,)owson, Wilde, and Rupert Brooke. Fitzgerald be-ame interested in these post-Romantics through ohn Peale Bishop, just as Amory became interested them through Thomas Park D'Invilliers. Bishop, in ict, was imitating Swinburne's poetry and eventually ublished a derivative collection entitled *Green Fruit* 1917), most of which had appeared in the *Nassau iterary Magazine.*

In *This Side of Paradise,* Amory tells us he is eading Swinburne: "The world became pale and nteresting, and he tried to look at Princeton through he satiated eyes of Oscar Wilde and Swinburne" 51]. This is an interesting remark because ten pages reviously we see Amory one night sadly looking at rinceton through Swinburnian eyes [41]. Fitzgerald most certainly depicting himself when he describes mory warming to Swinburne's sad and twilight verse bout the cult of youth and the rush of time, the ipening fruit and the sense of decay, yesterday's dim un and tonight's languid moon. Amory quotes Swin-urne's poetry from heart, especially the passage in *tlanta in Calydon* about "winter rains and ruins . . and time remembered is grief forgotten."[23] The heme and tone in *This Side of Paradise* are similar to uch other Swinburne poems as "Dolores" ("For the rown of our life as it closes/Is darkness, the fruit thereof dust," [95]), and the more pagan poem "Hymn to Prosperpine" ("Thou has conquered, (pale Galilean; the world has grown grey from th breath / . . . Laurel is green for a season, and love i sweet for a day;/But grows bitter with treason, and laurel outlives not May" [59]).

In *This Side of Paradise* Amory is also reading Walter Pater [cf. 106], and here again we find a important influence on Fitzgerald's developing imag nation. The emphasis that Fitzgerald puts upon youth is the same emphasis we find in *Marius the Epicurean* This personal history breaks into four parts. Pater firs traces Marius' boyhood and school life; he then show Marius becoming an Epicurean of the Cyrenai school which extols the moments of youth; he nex shows him becoming disillusioned with the Cyrenai philosophy, and he leaves him on the doorstep o Christianity, deeply attracted to the esthetics of the new religion but still without the faith to believe. The second stage of Marius' career, his belief in Cyrenai cism, leads him to a state of mind which he share with most of Fitzgerald's characters. In fact, wha Pater says of Marius could be taken, without qualifica tion, to describe Jay Gatsby.

> Thus the boyhood of Marius passed; on the whol more given to contemplation than to action. Les prosperous in fortune than at an earlier day there had been reason to expect . . . he lived much in the realn of the imagination, and became betimes, as he was to continue all through life, something of an idealist constructing the world for himself in great measure from within, by the exercise of meditative power. . . [He had an] innate and habitual longing for a world altogether fairer than that he saw.[24]

As Gatsby created in his imagination a world that die not exist, Marius does also. And as Gatsby idealizes Daisy Fay so Marius also had "the ideal of a perfec imaginative love, centered upon a type of beauty entirely flawless and clean" [76].

If there is in *Marius the Epicurean* a description o

Jay Gatsby, Ernest Dowson's "The Princess of Dreams" can be read as a summary of the novel as a whole. The parallelism between the two works is truly astonishing. In Dowson's prose poem the hero returns with newly amassed treasures to a beautiful girl whom he once loved, but he fails to regain her love, and he is defeated at the hands of a cruel and "slow witted" person, a guardian of her tower. The hero disappears, and the poem ends with the suggestion that the golden "princess" is fraudulently unworthy of the hero's fate.

THE PRINCESS OF DREAMS

Poor legendary princess! In her enchanted tower of ivory, the liberator thought that she awaited him.

For once in a dream he had seen, as they were flowers de luce, the blue lakes of her eyes, had seemed to be enveloped in a tangle of her golden hair.

And he sought her through the countless windings of her forest for many moons, sought her through the morasses, sparing not his horse nor his sword. On his way he slew certain evil magicians and many of his friends, so that at his journey's end his bright sword was tarnished and his comeliness swart with mud. His horses he had not spared; their bones made a white track behind him in the windings of the forest: but he still bore her ransom, and the costly, graceful things stored in a cypress chest: massed pearls and amethysts and silks from Samarcand, Valance of Venice, and fine tapestry of Tyre. All these he brought with him to the gates of her ivory tower.

Poor legendary princes.

For he did not free her and the fustian porter took his treasure and broke his stained sword in two.

And who knows where he went, horseless and dis-armed, through the morasses and the dark windings of her forest under the moonless night, dreaming of those blue lakes which were flowers de luce, her eyes? Who knows? For the fustian porter says nothing, being slow of wit.

But there are some who say that she had no wish to

be freed, and that those flowers de luce, her eyes, are a
stagnant, dark pool, that her glorious golden hair was
only long enough to reach her postern gate.

Some say, moreover, that her tower is not of ivory
and that she is not even virtuous nor a princess.[25]

There can be little doubt that Fitzgerald read "The
Princess of Dreams." Dowson is one of Amory
Blaine's favorite poets [cf. 51], and Dowson's life—his
six-year love for the young Adelaide Foltinowicz, the
daughter of a Polish immigrant who broke his heart
when she married a waiter in her father's restaurant—
would certainly have interested him. In *The Pierrot of
the Minute*, Dowson describes a man, a fool of time,
who becomes enslaved by his image of a beautiful
woman (a "Moon Maiden") and will forever be
under her spell. Daisy Fay could be speaking to
Gatsby when, in Dowson's poem, the lady tells her
lover:

> . . . *all thy days are mine, dreamer of dreams,*
> *All silvered over with the moon's pale beams:*
> *Go forth and seek in each fair face in vain,*
> *To find the image of thy love again.*
> *All maids are kind to thee, yet never one*
> *Shall hold thy truant heat till day be done.*
> *Whom once the moon has kissed, loves long and late,*
> *Yet never finds the maid to be his mate.*
> *Farewell, dear sleeper, follow out thy fate.* [179]

Dowson's poetic characters become the victims of
their imagination—and of time. Like all of Fitzgerald's heroes, they desire to arrest time, perpetuate the
moment, and enjoy forever the splendor of youth. As
one of Dowson's lovers puts it:

> *O could this moment be perpetuate!*
>   *Must we grow old, and leaden-eyed and gray,*
> *And taste no more the wild and passionate*
> *Love sorrows of to-day?*
>
> *Grown old, and faded, Sweet! and past desire,*
>   *Let memory die, lest there be too much ruth,*

Remembering the old, extinguished fire
Of our divine, lost youth. [90]

The jump from Ernest Dowson to Rupert Brooke is a short one. Brooke's father was an assistant master at Rugby where Brooke was educated and where, when he was seventeen, he met John Lucas, eight years his senior, a local poet, and a graduate of Oxford. Lucas was very interested in the decadent movement and, as Christopher Hassall tells us, "the poems of Dowson must have been among the first books that Lucas left with Rupert." [26] Lucas also introduced Brooke to Baudelaire, Gautier, Oscar Wilde, Walter Pater, and Swinburne. With its sense of languor, vague regret, and self-induced nostalgia for some lost love, Gautier's ideas had influenced Pater and the art for art's sake movement at Oxford and the poetry of the nineties.

Fitzgerald took the title *This Side of Paradise* from Brooke's poetry (". . . Well this side of Paradise! . . . There's little comfort in the wise"), prefaced the novel with a quote from Brooke, and referred five times to Amory's interest in Brooke's poetry [cf. 106, 118, 147, 231, and 280]. Amory even "tried to play Rupert Brooke as long as he knew Eleanor" [231]. Fitzgerald wrote Edmund Wilson (September 26, 1917) that he had a "literary month . . . (July) . . . [writing] a terrific lot of poetry mostly under the . . . Brooke influence" [317], and later Fitzgerald wrote that Brooke also influenced *The Romantic Egoist*.[27] In a letter to his Cousin Ceci written at the same time (June 10, 1917), Fitzgerald says that "it looks as if the youth of me and my generation end[ed] sometime during the present year. . . . If we ever get back . . . we'll be rather aged. . . . After all, life hasn't much to offer except youth and I suppose for older people the love of youth in others. I agree perfectly with Rupert Brooke's men of Grantchester:

> " 'Who when they to feeling old
> They up and shoot themselves I'm told.' " [28]

Brooke died from blood poisoning when he wa
only twenty-seven (on board a French hospital ship a
Scyros, April 23, 1915), and his death strangel
reinforced his poetic insistence upon youth's tragi
destiny. In his poetry, Brooke described yout
haunted by old age and time. "I'll curse the thing tha
once you were," the narrator in "The Beginning" say
to his lost love, "Because it is changed and pale an
old. . . . I loved you . . . When the flame o
youth was strong in your eyes,/And my heart is sic
with memories." [29] Brooke sings of a lost golden worl
and bewails the passage of the years which destroy
white Helen's perfect beauty:

. . . her golden voice
Got shrill as [Menelaus] grew deafer. And both wer
old. [74]

Everyone of Fitzgerald's novels, in one way o
another, ends on this note. Amory Blaine feels he ha
lost Rosalind forever because he "had wanted he
youth." He rejected "this Rosalind, harder, older-
nor any beaten, broken woman that his imaginatio
brought to the door of her forties" [253]. Anthon
Patch looks disgustedly at himself in the mirror
"contemplating dejectedly the wan, pasty face, . .
[the] lines . . . the stooped and flabby figure. . .
He was thirty-three—he looked forty" [444]. Ja
Gatsby realizes that the present is forever divorce
from the past, that "he had lost the old warm world'
[162]. And Dick Diver shares this feeling because h
"was not young any more with a lot of nice thought
and dreams to have about himself" [311].

The sentiments of Fitzgerald's characters can b
found in the novels as well as the poetry of the lat
nineteenth and early twentieth century. When h
refers to the "quest" novels with their disillusione
young heroes [cf. 120], Amory has H. G. Wells i
mind, a novelist whom Fitzgerald admits influence
This Side of Paradise.[30] In novels like *Tono-Bungay*

he New Machiavelli, and *The Research Magnifi-
ent,* a young hero suffers disappointment in love and
narriage, sees his values eroded in a fraudulent so-
iety, rejects the gods of the past, joins or becomes
nterested in the socialist movement, and is overcome
y a sense of cultural waste and purposelessness. In
ono-Bungay, for example, George Ponderevo origi-
ally wants "to serve and do and make—with some
obility. It was in me [he says]. It is in half the youth
f the world." [31] Instead he helps his uncle amass a
ortune by manufacturing Tono-Bungay, a worthless
atent medicine that is even injurious to its users. He
eels ashamed and guilty at his own success and
espondently concludes: "This irrational muddle of a
ommunity in which we live . . . paid [my uncle]
or sitting in a room and scheming and telling it lies.
'or he created nothing, he invented nothing, he
conomised nothing. . . . Yet it seems to me indeed
t times that all this present commercial civilization is
o more than my poor uncle's career writ large"
258–61].

In *The New Machiavelli,* which Amory reads at
'rinceton [cf. 118–19], the young hero, the son of a
cience teacher, is well educated at Cambridge, goes
n a walking tour through Switzerland, becomes
isenchanted with Europe's "functionless property
wners," dabbles in and then renounces socialism, is
narried and later divorced (a biographical fact that
Vells puts into most of his novels), runs successfully
or Parliament, comes to feel the need for eugenic
eform so that there will be "a great race mind behind
he interplay of individual lives," [32] continues with an
xtra-marital affair knowing it will bring social dis-
;race, and ends with the feeling that all "his Gods are
ead" [462]. Amory's sense of disillusionment, his
udden interest is socialism, his feeling that he had
;rown "to find all Gods dead," his final sense of
utility and vague humanitarian commitment—all of
hese elements Fitzgerald found in Wells, who was

very much within the Romantic tradition. Even Wells's socialism is within the boundaries of Romanticism. Through the political writings of Saint-Simon, Fourier, Owen, and Ruskin, the Romantic and esthetic writers were introduced to the political ideals of socialism long before Marx or Proudhon had their influence. Swinburne, Brooke, Oscar Wilde, along with Wells give to socialism the same consent that Amory Blaine and even Anthony Patch give, although this element is not completely assimilated in *This Side of Paradise*.

Even though *This Side of Paradise* owes much to both Rupert Brooke and H. G. Wells, Amory at the end of the novel rejects them as "evil" because they are preoccupied with sex. He extends his attack to include what seems to be the esthetic movement in general and all those who are interested in the beautiful for its own sake. After this, Amory begins thinking about the Catholic Church where the beauty of the ritual is not an end in itself. What is interesting here is that, like Amory's socialism, his newfound interest in Catholicism is also in keeping with the spirit of the esthetic poets—that is, with the spirit of Swinburne, Dowson, and Oscar Wilde—all of whom were attracted or converted to Catholicism. Amory even tells Eleanor that "like Napoleon and Oscar Wilde and the rest of your type, you'll yell loudly for a priest on your death-bed" [239].

The reference to Wilde is significant, especially because Fitzgerald turned to Wilde and Brooke for the title page quotations in *This Side of Paradise*. For the early Wilde there were two values in life—youth and beauty—and, logically enough, two enemies—old age and ugliness. As Lord Henry tells Dorian Gray:

> When your youth goes, your beauty will go with it, and then you will suddenly discover that there are no triumphs left for you, or have to content yourself with those mean triumphs that the memory of your past will make more bitter than defeats. Every month as it wanes

brings you nearer to something dreadful. Time is jealous of you, and wars against your lilies and your roses. You will become sallow, and hollow-cheeked, and dull-eyed. You will suffer horribly. Ah! realize your youth while you have it. Don't squander the gold of your days, listening to the tedious, trying to improve the hopeless failure, or giving away your life to the ignorant, the common, and the vulgar. . . . For there is such a little time that your youth will last—such little time. . . . In a month there will be purple stars on the clematis, and year after year the green night of its leaves will hold its purple stars. But we never get back our youth.[33]

The Picture of Dorian Gray is a *tour de force* inversion of "Ode on a Grecian Urn." Dorian, who wanted to "keep the unsullied splendour of eternal youth" [398], exists like an art object, outside and not subject to time. His portrait, on the other hand, exists like men, its beauty subject to the destructive forces of age and the ugly effects of a cruel and dissipated life. Wilde believed that there were no moral connections between life and art. As an "art object," Dorian Gray is independent of time, free of moral restrictions, and unaffected by events—including his own behavior. Wilde has pushed beyond Romantic idealism and allowed esthetics to absorb ethics, insisting that moral laws become irrelevant in the face of the beautiful. This leads us to the philosophy of the dandy whose pursuit of the beautiful is contingent upon the life of leisure and comfort and whose desire for luxury inculcated a contempt for the coarse and the ugly as well as the mundane and the purely materialistic. In *This Side of Paradise*, Monsignor Darcy, Thomas D'Invilliers (who introduces Amory to *The Picture of Dorian Gray*), and Amory himself are all dandies. They love comfort, are self-indulgent (the Monsignor to a lesser degree), appreciate the beautiful, and are cynical of and indifferent to a work-a-day world. " 'I'm tres old and tres bored,' " Amory tells Tom. " 'I

believe too much in the responsibilities of authorship
to write just now, and business, well, business speaks
for itself. It has no connection with anything in the
world that I've ever been interested in. . . . [I have
no desire to become] lost in a clerkship, for the next
and best ten years of my life' " [212, 216]. Anthony
Patch adopts this attitude verbatim, and he is a much
better illustration of Wilde's dandy. Fitzgerald himself uses the word to describe Anthony:

> He became an exquisite dandy, amassed a rather
> pathetic collection of silk pajamas, brocaded dressing
> gowns, and neckties too flamboyant to wear; in this
> secret finery he would parade before his mirror in his
> room or lie stretched in satin along his window seat
> looking down on the yard and realizing dimly this
> clamor, breathless and immediate, in which it seemed
> he was never to have a part." [8]

There has been a tendency to see Fitzgerald completely under the influence of H. L. Mencken's cynicism while he was writing *The Beautiful and
Damned*.[34] While Mencken had an influence, Fitzgerald was also deeply influenced by the portrait of the
dandy. Surprisingly, the novel that influenced him the
most was Frank Norris' *Vandover and the Brute*.
Both Amory and Fitzgerald were impressed with this
novel,[35] and the parallels between Anthony and Vandover are indeed striking. Both graduate from Harvard; Anthony has pretentions of becoming a writer,
Vandover of becoming an artist; both have delicate
tastes, enjoy the life of luxurious leisure, and appreciate manifestations of the beautiful; both are exquisite dressers, recognize good wine and music, and are
men-about-town; both are contemptuous of the business world, feel it is beneath them, and fail in their
slight attempts to make money; both enjoy a select
group of friends and each is betrayed by a member of
this group; both have disastrous love affairs with girls
socially beneath them, although otherwise each is

nobbisly contemptuous of the masses; and, finally, both are the victims of dissipation and physical decline. The passages describing this decline are very similar in tone and attitude:

The Beautiful and Damned:	Vandover and the Brute:
He had been futile in longing to drift and dream; no one drifted except to maelstroms, no one dreamed, without his dreams becoming fantastic nightmares of indecision and regret. [282]	He had no pleasures, no cares, no ambitions, no regrets, no hopes. It was mere passive existence, an inert, plantlike vegetation, the moment's pause before the final decay, the last inevitable rot. [36]

The description of Anthony in his New York apartment is also remarkably similar to Vandover in his San Francisco apartment [cf. *The Beautiful and Damned*, 10–12 and *Vandover and the Brute*, 181] as is the routine of Anthony and Vandover at their toilet [cf. *The Beautiful and Damned*, 17 and *Vandover and the Brute*, 102].

Fitzgerald, however, renounces the life of the dandy. At the end of Oscar Wilde's novel, Dorian Gray rejects the realm of art by rejecting his beauty ("he loathed his own beauty") and his youth ("his youth [became] a mockery"). When he destroys the picture, he destroys himself—that is, he destroys the autonomy of art which he himself embodies. For Wilde, art was anterior to an independent of life. This was not true for Fitzgerald. At the end of *This Side of Paradise*, Amory rejects the idea that beauty can exist independently of evil—a rejection, that is, of the main assumption in *The Picture of Dorian Gray*. And at the end of *The Beautiful and Damned*, Richard Caramel, Fitzgerald's alter-ego, rejects Anthony's suggestion that moral values exist in neither life nor art. As long as youth and beauty were subject to time,

Fitzgerald knew—unlike Anthony and Jay Gatsby—that one was morally responsible for the way he used time. One could neither relive the past nor expect the beauty of the moment to abide forever. Those who did were both mistaken and damned.

Ever since James E. Miller's *The Fictional Technique of Scott Fitzgerald*, we have been aware that Joseph Conrad had a major literary influence on Fitzgerald. The assumption, however, has been that Fitzgerald went to Conrad because he wanted to move from the novel of "saturation" to the novel of "selection" and that Fitzgerald saw in Conrad's Marlow a way of securing narrative compression at the same time as he established a distance between himself and his characters. This point can hardly be disputed, but no one has ever noticed that there is an affinity of mind—a common theme—which also connects Fitzgerald and Conrad.

In his Introduction to the Modern Library edition of *The Great Gatsby* (1934), Fitzgerald tells us that he reread Conrad's Preface to *The Nigger of the "Narcissus"* while he was writing his novel. For this reason, Conrad's Preface is widely quoted by those interested in Fitzgerald's developing literary technique. But in his Preface Conrad says that the artist "speaks to" and helps create "our capacity for delight and wonder, to the sense of mystery surrounding our lives." [37] Conrad, in other words, admits that he is a Romantic, excited by the man with the heightened conception of self.

Fitzgerald was well aware of this element in Conrad's fiction. In an article that he wrote for *The Literary Review of the New York Evening Post* (May 26, 1923), Fitzgerald quoted the following passage from Conrad's "Youth":

"I did not know how good a man I was till then . . . I remember my youth and the feeling that will never come back any more—the feeling that I could last forever, outlast the sea, the earth, and all men . . . the triumphant conviction of strength, the beat of life in the handful of dust, the glow in the heart that with every year grows dim, grows cold, grows small, and expires too soon—before life itself."

Fitzgerald then continued: "So, in part, runs one of the most remarkable passages of English prose written these thirty years."

Fitzgerald overstated his case, but his excitement is perhaps justified by the "remarkable" similarity of narrative pattern between his and Conrad's fiction. Like Fitzgerald, Conrad also saw youth as a moment of illusion—of promise and expectancy—which dims with age and which is often betrayed by experience. In "Youth," Marlow related his first voyage as a second mate, assigned to the *Judea* which was carrying a load of coal to Bangkok, the exciting East. There are a series of disasters—the ship is gutted, dry-docked, gets to sea where the coal catches fire, and finally explodes as it approaches its destination. Through it all, Marlow never loses his sense of romance and glamor. The story, of course, is ironic, for Marlow is the retrospective narrator who looks back over the years, recaptures the feeling of youth, and nostalgically longs for the past. Like Gatsby, Marlow has immortalized a moment of time which has led to a heightened conception of self: " 'For me,' " he says, " 'all the East is contained in that vision of my youth.' " [38] And as Fitzgerald used Nick Carraway to complement Gatsby's feeling of loss, Conrad used a narrator to introduce us to Marlow—a narrator who is also moved by Marlow's regret for his lost youth:

"And we all nodded at [Marlow]: . . . we all . . . looking anxiously for something out of life, that while it is expected is already gone—has passed unseen, in a sigh, in a flash—together with the youth, with the strength, with the romance of illusions." [42]

In "Youth," Marlow is unable even to intuit the terror and the horror that exists in Conrad's world. He is blinded by his innocence and has not yet reached the point—the shadow-line—where he is aware of the catastrophe to which frail man is subject, or the evil that exists in others, or the evil that is latent in his own heart. Most of Conrad's characters better understand themselves by seeing that others are evil or frail —as Almayer sees evil in Lakamba, as Willems (in *An Outcast of the Island*) sees it in Aissa, as Lord Jim sees it in Brown (in this case after he has seen it first in himself), as Marlow (in "The Heart of Darkness") sees it in Kurtz, and as Heyst (in *Victory*) sees it in Ricardo. Conrad's characters are tormented and lonely men, plagued by grief, and wracked with guilt. They are often in flight from themselves, modern-day Cains, whose crimes have alienated them from society. Some are destroyed by their encounter with "the destructive element" (Almayer, Willems, Kurtz, Decoud and Nostromo, Mr. Verloc and Winnie), while others are morally strengthened by their ordeal, even though it at times costs their lives (Lord Jim, Rasumov, Flora de Barral, and Heyst). Sometimes those who are saved are helped back by the love of someone else as Aissa helps Willems (although her love finally turns to destructive jealousy), as Nathalie helps Razumov in *Under Western Eyes*, as Anthony helps Flora in *Chance*, and as Lena helps Heyst in *Victory*. In all cases, those who are saved have undergone a change; they have pealed away all their early illusions, abandoned their hopeless dreams, and accepted themselves for what they are and can do. The man of illusions immerses himself in the destructive element, and he is sustained by his dreams at the same time as the dream is tempered by experience. " 'Woe to the man whose heart has not learned while young to hope, to love—and to put its trust in life,' " says Heyst.[39] Conrad's characters must first lose themselves in order to find themselves.

Conrad thus goes beyond the Romantic to the tragic vision and reveals the human limitations which are both the source of man's plight and the beginning of his newfound strength and self-understanding. If Marlow in "Youth" never overcomes naïveté, two other stories—"The Secret Sharer" and *The Shadow-Line*—reveal the hero gradually and then finally aware of the destructive element.

"The Secret Sharer" was published in 1912 in the collection entitled *'Twixt Land and Sea*. The young captain, in charge of his first ship, is very much a Romantic visionary with a heightened conception of self. In fact, he ponders at the beginning "how far I should turn out faithful to that ideal conception of one's own personality every man sets up for himself secretly." [40]

He finds out that he is really a "stranger" to himself in a "homeless" world when he helps a fugitive—a typical Conradian outcast, the "brand of Cain" upon him—who in a fit of rage murdered a "miserable devil" aboard the *Sephora* because he "wouldn't do his duty and wouldn't let anybody else do theirs" [101]. The mate escaped from imprisonment by diving overboard, was chased naked through a chain of islands by the crew of the *Sephora*, and began his hopeless swim which took him to the young captain's ship when he thought it was taking him to his death. The captain feels complicity in the mate's murder, sees him as his "double," and is attracted to the fugitive "as if our experiences had been as identical as our clothes" [102]. The young captain has passed through "the gate of everlasting night," has seen the illusions and egotism of youth give way to human solidarity, and has realized that his old self has been enlarged—has grown and changed—because of his new compassion, because of his sympathy and "pity for his [the fugitive's] mere flesh" [142]. He is saved by this compassion when the hat he thrust upon the mate, to protect him from the sun, falls off and bobs in the current, serving as the marker which saves the ship from crashing upon the rocks.

The Shadow-Line, published in 1917, is very similar in pattern and meaning to "Youth." The story opens with these words:

> Only the young have such moments. . . . It is the privilege of early youth to live in advance of its days in all the beautiful continuity of hope which knows no pauses and no introspection.
> . . . *It's very shades glow with promise.*[41]

This sense of youthful promise, however, also gives way to an understanding of man's frailty and tragic humanity. The hero of *The Shadow-Line* is a young seaman who deserts his ship because he is restless at sea. As he waits in an Officer's Club for passage home, he accepts the command of a ship whose captain has recently died. Once at sea, fever levels the crew and officers of his ship, except for the young captain himself and a Mr. Ransome, the cook, who has a bad heart and could not sign aboard for more strenuous work. The first mate, Mr. Burns, is haunted by the death of the old captain whom they buried at sea—at latitude 8°20′ North—the entrance of the Gulf of Siam (exactly where the captain in "Youth" picks up the young fugitive). Mr. Burns fears the captain's spirit is haunting the ship and will destroy them all. Like the fever, Burns's fears become contagious—at least to the new captain. As a storm approaches, he loses his youthful sanguineness and sees the ship as "a bottomless black pit" in a "blackness which had swallowed up our world" [110]. During the storm even the binnacle lights go out—"the last gleam of light in the universe" [114]. As Burns raves in his fever about the evils of the old captain, the new one—assisted by Ransome—tries to steer a "wildly rushing ship full of dying men" [124]. The ship metaphorically is the Conradian universe, where men labor against the elements as well as sickness, madness, and death. In their struggle, the young captain sees in Ransome the source of both man's tragic weakness and strength. He becomes aware of the delicate line (the shadow-line) between life and death. He suddenly realizes that all men, like Ransome, have weak hearts—a heart which allows us the dignity of struggle, a heart that binds us together, and a heart that can betray us at any moment. Our strength—like Ransome's tragic strength—is really in our weakness.

When Conrad's youths become aware of this truth, they become men. Conrad's characters—such as Lord Jim, Nostromo, Razumov, Flora de Barral, for example —recognize their mistakes in judgment, accept their limits, and find enough strength, even when confronted with death, to expiate the past. Fitzgerald's boy-men, on the other hand, never really grow up. They usually feel victimized, retreat into self-pity, and fade away in defeat. The difference between a Gatsby and a Lord Jim is that Jim becomes more realistic, is strengthened by his defeat, and makes his ordeal a way of life. The difference, in other words, is between a Romantic and a tragic view of man. While Conrad and Fitzgerald began at the same Romantic starting point, Conrad moved into a darker realm of life—a realm which Fitzgerald was emotionally unable to accept or to depict.

Lost in the depths of Malayan or African jungles, isolated upon the sea, garreted in the slums of Soho, Conrad's characters pit their will against the elements and struggle with the barbarity they find in others— and in themselves. While for Conrad the forces of evil are usually both inside and out, the conflict for Fitzgerald is too often merely an external one. Fitzgerald's characters are usually misused by others before they are overwhelmed by the passing of time. Their decline seems inevitable and fated. Fascinated by the process of deterioration and decline, Fitzgerald naturally gravitated to the writing of Oswald Spengler whose influence on his works is so great that it is amazing it has so long been overlooked. In a letter to Maxwell Perkins, Fitzgerald tells us of his interest in Spengler.

"I read him the same summer I was writing *The Great Gatsby* and I don't think I ever quite recovered from him. He and Marx are the only modern philosophers that still manage to make sense in this horrible mess — I mean make sense by themselves and not in the hands of distorters. Even Mr. Lenin looks now like a much better politician than a philosopher. Spengler, on the other hand, prophesied gang rule, 'young peoples hungry for spoil,' and more particularly 'the world as spoil' as an idea, a dominant supercessive idea." [42]

Although Spengler rejected the idea of teleology and progress, the historical theories developed in *The Decline of the West* are very much a part of the Romantic tradition. Spengler himself acknowledged two influences on his work. One was Goethe's theory of *Urphäneomen*—the belief in cultural morphology, that each civilization has a prime phenomenon, a cultural essence which distinguishes it from other periods of history. The other influence was Nietzsche's idea of "eternal recurrence"—the belief that all things would eventually return to their origin and that the cycle of life would be repeated.

Spengler believed that the laws of biology were also the laws of history. Each culture was an organism which had a pattern of birth, growth, maturity, and decay. He concentrated on three stages of Western history—the Apollinian or classical period, the Magian or medieval realm, and the Faustian or modern age. The Apollinian period finds man generally self-satisfied; their art and literature show an interest in body and form and a belief that the meaning can be circumscribed and truths clearly defined. The Magian period, which begins to emerge in the decades before the birth of Christ, finds man torn between forces of good and evil and interested in the power of magic. The Faustian period, Spengler's main concern, begins around the tenth century with papal reform, and finds man longing for the unattainable. Spengler believed that there were logical explanations for Apollinian man inventing geometry (which reveals his interest in magnitude), Magian man, algebra (which reveals his interest in relationship), and Faustian man, calculus (which reveals his interest in infinity). The nude was to Apollinian art, Spengler maintained, what the fugue was to Faustian art. The Apollinian period was static; the Faustian, dynamic. Spengler believed that the shift from the countryside to the city after the Reformation marked the loss of Faustian man's youth —the passing of his cultural spring and summer; that the eighteenth century was the autumn of the Faustian age; and that the nineteenth century was the beginning of western man's wintry decline. During the decline there would be the rise of the megalopolis (like New York and Berlin), a growing uniformity as the machine age relegated man to a routine of dull tasks, and the triumph of money over aristocracy. Spengler dreaded the coming of the "monied thugs," and "new Caesars," who would destroy the last Faustian men. In England and America, where the main distinction is between rich and poor, the new Caesar would be a cruel materialist—a millionaire, a banker, a man of wealth and success. In Germany, where the main distinction is between command and obedience, the new Caesar would be a dictator—a general, a high official, a man of authority and power. After the rise and triumph of such figures, they would in turn be overthrown by the rise of the "colored" races—by which Spengler meant the Negroes and Chinese, and also the Russians (whom he considered to be a part of the Orient) —races that would use the technology of the West to destroy its inventors.

Fitzgerald worked a surprising number of these Spenglerian elements into *The Great Gatsby*. Tom

Buchanan is very much a "monied thug," a new Caesar. Cruel and careless, he reveals the degeneration that has taken place in the old order—that is, the old aristocracy. In this connection, Nick Carraway significantly tells us at the very beginning of the novel that he is from a family that has an aristocratic background: "The Carraways are something of a clan, and we have a tradition that we're descended from the Dukes of Buccleuch" [2]. Consistent with Spengler's theory of history, the old values which Nick attributes to his father (and which Fitzgerald predicated of his own father) have been replaced by the unscrupulous methods of the monied Buchanans. These methods destroy Gatsby—one of the last Fausts, a man of infinite desires who longs for the unattainable. Nick's retreat from the East, the center of commerce, reveals his desire to return to the old pastoral world, a world that Spengler associated with the Faustian period of "youth." New York has for Nick (as it had for Fitzgerald) all the excitement of youth, and at one point Nick describes it in pastoral terms: "We drove over to Fifth Avenue," he says, "so warm and soft, almost pastoral, on the summer Sunday afternoon that I wouldn't have been surprised to see a great flock of white sheep turn the corner" [28]. Appearance here belies reality, as it does throughout the novel, and it is only at the end that Nick realizes the pastoral realm— and the spirit of youth which Spengler predicated of it —has been consumed in the rush—Spengler would say the "cycles"—of time. Nick's flight also reveals that he has been defeated by the Buchanans—by the new Caesars—and his persistent reference to the push of history, the loss of the glorious past, the end of the frontier, all suggest a Spenglerian attitude toward time.

An understanding of Spengler is also the key to a number of other passages in *The Great Gatsby*. At one point, Tom Buchanan asks Nick if he has read " *The Rise of the Colored Empires* by this man

Goddard?' " [13] [45] Goddard's book troubles Tom Buchanan because it predicts the end of his class structure and the rise of Spengler's "colored races":

> "Well, it's a fine book, [says Tom] and everybody ought to read it. The idea is if we don't look out the white race will be—will be utterly submerged. It's all scientific stuff; it's been proved." [13]

Tom is a bore, and no one takes him seriously. Yet, interestingly enough, as Gatsby and Nick are driving from Long Island to New York, crossing Blackwell's Island, a limousine passes them, "driven by a *white* chauffeur, in which sat three modish *negroes*, two bucks and a girl" [69, italics mine]. The inversion of race and class relations—the Negroes owning the limousine, the white man their hired driver—suggests that the next stage in Spengler's historical process is already under way. It also suggests that Fitzgerald worked into *The Great Gatsby* the three stages of the Faustian realm: Faustian man (Gatsby) gives way to the "new Caesars" (Tom Buchanan), who in turn gives way to the rising colored races. The passing of the Buchanans will mark the final decline of the Western world—the shift of power from the West to the East. Fitzgerald makes great use of the juxtaposition between West and East in *The Great Gatsby*, even concluding the novel with these words: "I see now [says Nick] that this has been a story of the West, after all—Tom and Gatsby, Daisy and Jordan and I, were all Westerners" [177].

Fitzgerald also introduced as many Spenglerian elements in *Tender Is the Night* as he did in *The Great Gatsby*. The degenerating Warren family reveals the decay of the aristocracy because Nicole "was the granddaughter of the House of Lippe Weissenfeld" [53]. As "the granddaughter of a self-made American capitalist" [53], she seems also to embody the rise of Spengler's monied class. Much of the novel takes place in Geneva, Switzerland, "on the centre of

the lake, cooled by the piercing current of the Rhône,
[where] lay the true centre of the Western World"
[147]. Into the "center" of this world steps Tommy
Barban who seems to be a composite of Spenglerian
elements. As both soldier and broker, he combines the
English and the Prussian characteristics of the new
Caesar. With truly international range, he preys upon
the waning aristocracy, and he gets stronger as they
get weaker. As he becomes more powerful, Tommy
moves beyond Spengler's idea of the Faustian destroyer, and his fate parallels the Spenglerian rise of
another civilization, another order. This is suggested
when Fitzgerald says that "his handsome face was so
dark as to have lost the pleasantness of deep tan"

[269]. Tommy is not a Negro, but Fitzgerald connects
him to Spengler's "colored races" by stating that he
"was less civilized" [19], by making him dark, and by
contrasting his dark skin with Dick's white complex-
ion. The night Nicole and Tommy become lovers, for
example, Nicole noticed that Tommy was "dark,
scarred and handsome . . . his figure was darker and
stronger than Dick's" [294]. And when Dick leaves
Gausse's beach for the last time, he is reluctant "to
look at those two other figures, a man and a woman
[Tommy and Nicole], black and white and metallic
against the sky" [313]. When Tommy Barban becomes Nicole's lover, when he replaces Dick as her
protector, a kind of savage—a barbarian, as his name
suggests—has usurped the place of the Faustian man
—the dreamer and the idealist—and has laid claim to
the very spirit, the physical embodiment of the Western world, because for Nicole's "sake, trains began
their run at Chicago and traversed the round belly of
the continent . . ..for her the whole system swayed
and thundered" [55]. Fitzgerald stylistically suggests
that Tommy's triumph is one of East over West when
he tells us that Nicole "symbolically . . . lay across
[Tommy's] saddlebow as surely as if he had wolfed
her away from Damascus and they had come out upon

the Mongolian plain" [297–98]. Thus, as in *The Great Gatsby*, Fitzgerald has shown the decay of the aristocracy, the degeneration of the monied class (symbolized by Devereux Warren's incest and Baby Warren's "onanistic" manner), and the rise of the new barbarian—the dark and militant intruder who conquers the West.

Fitzgerald reinforces the function of Tommy Barban in *Tender Is the Night* by having Mary North, a descendant of President Tyler [53], marry Conte di Minghetti, whose papal title fails to conceal the fact that "he was not quite light enough to travel in a pullman south of Mason-Dixon" [258], and that his wealth comes from Southwestern Asia. The decline of Dick Diver parallels the decline of the West—at least as Spengler envisioned such a decline. Dick is a Faustian man who falls before the "new Caesar" and the "colored races."

There is also a conflict between a new Caesar and a Faustian man in *The Last Tycoon*. When Kathleen describes her fiancé, she tells of how he tried to educate her by preparing long reading lists (as Fitzgerald prepared such lists for Sheilah Graham). " 'He wanted me to read Spengler,' " she tells Stahr, " 'everything was for that' " [91]. As one would suspect, Stahr does not recognize Spengler's name. Yet Stahr is very much Spengler's Faustian man, and much of the novel takes place in a context that suggests the deterioration of his world. Stahr, who is described as "a little like the Emperor and the Old Guard" [27], is linked with the old order; in fact, he is called "the last of the princes" [27], a phrase that is really more appropriate as the novel's title. Fitzgerald further links Stahr with the dying aristocratic order by juxtaposing him against Prince Agge, whose function in the novel is to express his awe of Hollywood and his dislike of the new Caesars, whom he calls "dull dogs" [46], a sentiment that complements Wylie White's dislike of such business barons as Gould, Vanderbilt,

Carnegie, and Astor [cf. 16]. Cecilia Brady's father is the embodiment of this new class, and he is one of Spengler's "monied thugs." As such, he is Stahr's mortal enemy—just as Tom Buchanan was Gatsby's and Tommy Barban was Dick Diver's. When he introduces us to the Communist Brimmer, who is morally stronger than both Stahr and Brady, Fitzgerald suggests a new threat to their security, the possibility of another turn in Spengler's cyclical system. As Brimmer says to Stahr, " 'you think [and you hope] the system will last out your time' " [122]. Stahr's destruction in *The Last Tycoon* is thus inevitable; he is doomed like Spengler's Faust.

With the publication of *The Great Gatsby*, Fitzgerald began to depict a civilization in decline, a social order that was running out of time. He was, of course, not the only modern writer depicting the decay of the old order, the inevitable end of the aristocracy in the postwar world. The deracinated and pitiful aristocrats that Fitzgerald depicts in *Tender Is the Night* have a great deal in common, after all, with Hemingway's Lady Brett and Mike Campbell, whom we usually forget have title and whose spiritual dereliction and moral bankruptcy reflects the status of the aristocratic class to which they belong. T. S. Eliot, of course, had previously caught the mood of this postwar world in *The Waste Land*, and Pound, questioning why young men should have died to keep such a *status quo*, wrote the epitaph in "Hugh Selwyn Mauberley":

> Died some, pro patria,
>   non 'dulce' non 'et decor'
> walked eye-deep in hell
> believing in old men's lies . . . .
> There dies a myriad
> And of the best, among them,
> For an old bitch gone in the teeth,
> For a botched civilization.

Dick Diver shares Pound's feelings. When Tommy Barban tells of how three Red guards were killed during Prince Chillicheff's escape from Russia, "Dick decided that this parched papier mâché relic of the past was scarcely worth the lives of three men" [198]. As Fitzgerald's feelings about his father fluctuated between admiration and pathos, his feelings toward the dying aristocracy—which encouraged the Tommy Barbans, the very agents of their destruction—turned from admiration to scorn.

It was Van Wyck Brooks who first emphasized the schizophrenic culture in which the American writer functions with its conflict stemming from the irreconcilable differences between the transcendental idealist and the materialistic pragmatist. Emerson, a true Romantic, believed that God was a part of nature and that an impulse from nature was an impulse from God. Men should be true to themselves by being self-reliant and by living spontaneously and unencumbered close to nature. Thoreau's journey to Walden put Emerson's ideas into practice; he chose to be an outcast because he could not sanction the system that subordinated men to property and machines.

Thoreau's conflict was also Hawthorne's, whose early life was hermetic and who tried the Brook Farm experiment. It is not really surprising that in *The Scarlet Letter* Hester Prynne lives half way between the town and the forest, participating in the society at the same time as she is its outcast. After seven years of such tribulation, she is willing to forsake the benefits of her good deeds, to repeat the past, to give in to her heart, and run deeper into the forest with Dimmesdale. Pearl—or rather Hawthorne through Pearl— stops her, and final redemption takes place with Dimmesdale's public confession on the scaffold. Hawthorne suppresses the Romantic instinct and subordinates the individual to the community—albeit an imperfect community, just as man himself, because of original sin, is imperfect.

If Hawthorne frustrates the Thoreauvian idealist, Mark Twain allows him complete fulfillment. There is nothing to stop Huck from striking out for the territory ahead where he can continue to live by the dictates of his heart and where he can escape the social and religious laws that tell him a Negro is property and that he will go to Hell if he helps Jim escape.

Henry James's Christopher Newman in *The American* is also a moral pilgrim who rejects the system and goes in search of himself. His escape, however, is not into the frontier, the territory ahead, but into old Europe, the land that has been left behind. And he finds that the past is dead. The Bellegardes, the last vestiges of aristocracy, are totally corrupt (like the mother and the son), or the victims of their own impractical code of honor (like Valentin), or the pathetic pawn in a scheme to save the old order (like Claire). Newman's dilemma is a familiar one to Fitzgerald's heroes. Failing to realize (cf. Gatsby, Dick Diver, Monroe Stahr) or to find (cf. Amory Blaine, Anthony Patch) ideals, they end up in a cultural vacuum, unable to court once again the bitch-goddess success or to tolerate a world that has lost gentlemanly integrity.

The Romantic conflict in Fitzgerald's novels is thus not that of Thoreau. Thoreau rejected society—the "machine," as he called it—in the name of transcendental ideals. There is nothing spiritual or hieroglyphic in nature for Fitzgerald's characters whose ideals are social and whose disillusionment is predetermined by Fitzgerald's use of "Keatsian" time and by Spengler's historical assumptions. Fitzgerald, in other words, depicts a Faustian hero—a man of longing—whose very desires are self-destructive. Fitzgerald once said, "My view of life . . . is the view of the Theodore Dreisers and Joseph Conrads—that life is too strong and remorseless for the sons of men." [44] When one thinks of Sister Carrie, Clyde Griffiths, and even Cowperwood—yearning for more than they can pos-

sibly attain or keep, faithfully struggling within the
system they blindly accept—Fitzgerald's reference to
Dreiser is strangely apt. This is not to say that
Fitzgerald could ever accept Dreiser's naturalistic
assumptions, but Fitzgerald's "inverted" Romanticism—the destructive yearning of his characters, the
moth and the flame pattern of his fiction—brings
Fitzgerald at times close to Dreiser.

This same "inverted" Romanticism separates Fitzgerald from two of his more immediate contemporaries—Ernest Hemingway and William Faulkner.
Hemingway's characters are more obviously at home
in nature than Fitzgerald's. Nick Adams of *In Our
Time* is at peace in the Michigan woods; Jake Barnes
is happiest in the mountains close to the swift-running
trout streams, hearing the ripple of the tall pines,
feeling the sun hot in the blue, cloudless sky of Spain;
Lt. Henry and Catherine find a temporary sense of
well-being in the Alps; Robert Jordan refreshes himself in the cold mountain brooks and dries off under a
warm sun in the uncontaminated setting in *For
Whom the Bell Tolls*; and both Harry Morgan and
Santiago are at home on the bright, clear Gulf Stream.
While Hemingway's characters are at one with nature, they do not deify or spiritualize it, and they learn
through experience and not intuition. In fact, Hemingway's characters are suspect of ideals and abstrac-
tions ("I was always embarrassed by . . . abstract
words such as glory, honor, courage, or hallow," says
Lt. Henry),[45] and the values which exist are those that
the individual constructs and preserves himself. This
is the source of an important difference between
Hemingway and Fitzgerald. Fitzgerald's hero puts
everything to the test of an overactive imagination,
while Hemingway's hero puts it to the test of experience. Fitzgerald's hero gets weaker as he gets older,
while Hemingway's hero gets stronger; and Fitzgerald's
hero is overcome by his mistakes, while Hemingway's
hero learns from them and becomes wiser.

The difference between Hemingway and Fitzgerald,

to put this another way, is the difference between Fitzgerald's ultimate admiration of Gatsby and Hemingway's contempt for Robert Cohn. For Gatsby and Cohn are, indeed, very much alike. Both live in terms of an imaginative conception of self; both are knight errants living in an unreal world; and both fail to profit by experience. When Cohn tells Jake that hunting in British East Africa does not interest him, Jake responds:

> "Thats because you never read a book about it. Go on and read a book all full of love affairs with the beautiful shiny black princesses." [46]

One can envision Cohn reading such a book—and reading it as literally as he read W. H. Hudson's *The Purple Land*—just as one knows that Gatsby read and accepted Benjamin Franklin's dictums to the good and successful life.

While both Gatsby and Cohn live by derivative notions, both Jake Barnes and Lt. Henry live by existential values. In both *A Farewell to Arms* and *The Sun Also Rises*, the Hemingway hero stands between an idealist or absolutist (the priest in *Arms*, Cohn in *Sun*) and a nihilist (Rinaldi in *Arms* and Mike Campbell in *Sun*), rejecting the values of each because idealism leads to an untested conception of self, and nihilism leads to the moral abandonment of the syphilitic Rinaldi and the dipsomaniac Mike Campbell.

The Hemingway hero ultimately believes that all values are relative and that meaning must be created by man himself. To live in terms of absolutes is to court disillusionment. *A Farewell to Arms* is a study in twofold disillusionment—disillusionment in love and war. At the beginning of the novel, Lt. Henry thinks of war as if it were some glorious football game and that he is playing a totally necessary part; he is slightly disillusioned when he returns from leave and finds that all is running well without him [cf. 16]; he is more disillusioned when, behind the lines, eating a piece of cheese and drinking wine, he suffers his absurd and gratuitous wound [cf. 56–57]; and he is totally disillusioned and makes his "separate peace" when he is almost shot by Italians during the retreat from Caporetto [cf. 240–41]. If he idealizes war at the beginning of the novel, Lt. Henry has at this point no illusions about love. He encourags Catherine because she is beautiful and he sexually wants her, "This was better than going every evening to the house for officers" [31]; his attitude becomes less cynical as Catherine nurses him in the hospital and accompanies him on his leave; and he is truly and ideally in love with her when they escape from Italy and spend a kind of Edenic winter in the Alps. At this point, Lt. Henry has raised "love" to the same absolute realm that he had placed "war." When Catherine dies in childbirth, love, like war, is negated as an absolute. Lt. Henry is washed of all illusions, and A *Farewell to Arms* ends where *The Sun Also Rises* begins—with the hero trying to find a kind of existential meaning, a more realistic kind of commitment—in this indifferent universe.

Unlike Hemingway's hero, Fitzgerald's characters do not live in a kind of existential world, are not cut off from others by the "separate peace" or by the absurd wound, and seldom (as in the case of Jake Barnes and Santiago) have the capacity to go on in the face of defeat. And since meaning in fiction cannot be divorced from the language of fiction, the styles of Hemingway and Fitzgerald are also radically different. Fitzgerald's language reinforces a Gatsby's ideal world. The descriptive passages, in particular, suggest a dreamlike realm where the laws of nature are suspended. When Nick Carraway, for example, first sees Daisy and Jordan Baker, they are on an enormous couch "buoyed up as though upon an anchored balloon" [8]. When he first meets George Wilson, "a white ashen dust veiled his [Wilson's] dark suit and his pale hair as it veiled everything in the vicinity" [26]. And when Nick goes to Gatsby's party, one of the first guests he meets is a stout man "with enormous owl-eyed spectacles" who is surprised because the books in the library are "real" [45]. There is something grotesque, almost surrealistic, in Fitzgerald's description of New York as a "city rising up across the river in white heaps and sugar lumps all built with a wish out of non-olfactory money" [69]. Nick sees with eyes that are slightly out of focus and even the physically possible seems strange like Dr. T. J. Eckleburg's eyes, "blue and gigantic—their retinas one yard high" [23], and Fifth Avenue, "so pastoral" that Nick expects "to see a great flock of white sheep turn the corner" [28], and Gatsby's house, "on fire . . . with light, which fell unreal on the shrubbery" [82].

Fitzgerald creates an equally distorted and heightened world in *Tender Is the Night*. The beach in front of Gausse's Hotel becomes a "bright tan prayer rug" [3]. The dinner table rises "a little toward the sky like a mechanical dancing platform" [34]. And the heads of a trio of women look "like long-stemmed flowers and rather like cobras' hoods" [72]. Fitzgerald's use of color imagery, often contradictory colors, creates a further sense of the unreal. Nicole's face is "ivory gold" [141]; other women have "faces powdered pinkish gray" [150]; nights are "white"; twilights are "green and cream" [74]; and the sea is the color of "green milk, blue as laundry water, wine dark" [15]. Fitzgerald's prose, in other words, is inflated to create a moonlit, magically heightened world of youthful splendor.

If the key to Fitzgerald's style is overstatement, the key to Hemingway's is understatement. Hemingway never states but tries to suggest a character's emotion by describing physical objects which "correlate" with that emotion, such as his description of the coal barges moving high and empty down the Seine to

uggest Jake's feelings of loneliness when Brett stands
iim up, or the dirty coffee glasses and table to suggest
ake's feeling of complicity after Brett leaves the café
with Pedro Romero. Hemingway's characters are what
Albert Camus called American "innocents"; they are
entient and passive, respond behavioristically to immediate stimulus, and establish a one-to-one relation-
hip between themselves and the absurd world that
:ontains them. In the following passage, describing
ake and Bill Gorton walking in the Burguete country-
ide, we can see that Hemingway's style is perfectly in
iccord with the nature and the meaning of his
iovel.

We packed the lunch and two bottles of wine in the
rucksack, and Bill put it on. I carried the rod-case and
the landing-nets slung over my back. We started up the
road and then went across a meadow and went toward
the woods on the slope of the first hill. We walked
across the fields on the sandy path. The fields were
rolling and grassy and the grass was short from the
sheep grazing. The cattle were up in the hills. We
heard their bells in the woods.

The paths crossed a stream on a foot-log. The log was
surfaced off, and there was a sapling bent across for a
rail. In the flat pool beside the stream tadpoles spotted
the sand. We went up a steep bank and across the
rolling fields. Looking back we saw Burguete, white
houses and red roofs, and the white road with a truck
going along it and the dust rising.

Beyond the fields we crossed another faster-flowing
stream. A sandy road led down to the ford and beyond
into the woods. The path crossed the stream on another
foot-log below the ford, and joined the road, and we
went into the woods.

It was a beech woods and the trees were very old.
Their roots bulked above the ground and the branches
were twisted. We walked on the road between the thick
trunks of the old beeches and the sunlight came
through the leaves in the light patches on the grass. The
trees were big, and the foliage was thick but it was not
gloomy. There was no undergrowth, only the smooth

grass, very green and fresh, and the big gray trees wel
spaced as though it were a park. [116–17]

This passage reveals a simple mind at work upor
immediate experience. The language here creates a
sense of facticity, a sense of things as they are–
independent, separate, and distinct. Each sentence i
the statement of an empirical fact in relation to a
moment of time: a series of independent or correla
tive clauses reveals an unexpressed belief in a unilat
eral scheme of values and a gratuitous and absurc
order of being without hierarchy or causality. Jak
never gets beyond sensory fact, and there is a one-to
one relationship between the object of description anc
the emotions of the narrator. Jake is at home close to
nature; and he lyrically responds to the mountain air
the woods, the trout streams. The predominance o
nouns is important because the nouns reveal th
objects of excitement. As Hemingway has said, "th
real thing" is "the sequence of motion and fact whic
[makes] the emotion." The nouns are syntacticall
structured with anticipatory subjects, or with predicat
adjectives, emphasizing that the narrator first become
aware of things and then responds to their qualitie
For example, we have "the fields were rolling an
grassy," "the grass was short," "the log was surfacec
off," and "the trees were big, and the foliage wa
thick." The object of each sentence usually become
the subject of the next clause. Mind and emotion ar
caught up in the natural sequence of things.

As this passage clearly reveals, Jake Barnes live
concretely on the level of the senses. This is tru
throughout the novel. He is happy and excited on th
car trip through the rugged Spanish mountains. Rot
ert Cohn, on the other hand, very much a Jay Gatsb
lives once removed from reality in the autonomou
realm of his imagination, and he sleeps throughou
the whole trip [93]. In the mountains of Burguete
Jake is best able to cope with his situation because th
setting itself is a kind of "elemental reduction"–tha

, a simplification of life and behavior. In Paris and
'omplona, Jake is more bewildered and less sure of
imself because the setting is more chaotic and com-
lex. The complexity of Jake's mind is in direct
elationship with the complexity of his setting. He is
onditoned by his experiences; and while he never
opes with problems abstractly ("I did not care what
. was all about") [148], he is hardened by events
"All I wanted to know was how to live in it [the
vorld]") [148], and seems at the end much more
motionally compact. At least Hemingway suggests
hat Jake has put his emotions into some kind of order
y contrasting his early sentimentality (" 'Couldn't
'e live together, Brett? Couldn't we just live to-
ether?' " [55], with the way Jake undercuts Brett's
entimentality at the end (" 'Oh, Jake,' Brett said, 'we
ould have had such a damned good time together.'
. . 'Yes,' I said. 'Isn't it pretty to think so?' ") [247].
Iemingway's hero defines himself by his actions, goes
hrough a process of disillusionment, gains emotional
rength, and begins to see realistically. Fitzgerald's
ero defines himself by his expectations, goes through
process of disillusionment, loses his youth and his
outhful vitality, and forever looks through a glass
arkly.

As Fitzgerald's imagination is different from Hem-
igway's, so also it is different from William Faulk-
er's. Faulkner created in his major novels the narra-
vely coherent world—the moral realm—of Yoknapa-
iwpha County. There was once a harmony here, but
ie harmony and order was destroyed in the backwash
f time by a terrible deed—an original sin—which
imbled its people into chaos and disorder. This "sin"
f the past is connected generally to slavery and
articularly to miscegenation, often incestuous misce-
enation. At the center of Faulkner's greatest novels
id stories—*Absalom, Absalom!* and "The Bear,"
or example—is the act of incestuous miscegenation.
s in the novels of Hawthorne, Faulkner's novels

show how the sins of the father are passed down to
the sons; yesterday's acts become today's burdens. In
the very center of Yoknapatawpha County is the court
house, on the top of which is the clock, and in the
basement of which is the jail. Time becomes a prison
for Faulkner's characters—especially Quentin Comp
son, who sees the old families and stately mansions
deteriorating before his eyes and who believes that
such deterioration is the result of unexpiated events
which have contaminated at the source the spring of
both time and nature. If, as in Fitzgerald's fiction
time is a destructive process in Faulkner's novels, it is
not for the same reason. Fitzgerald sees time in
Keatsian and Spenglerian terms—man and civiliza
tions move from birth to death through a process of
growth and decay; the rose grows toward death as it
grows toward its moment of beautiful perfection
Faulkner, on the other hand, sees time in Hebraic
Christian terms—acts of the past have their effect in
the future; time past is contained in time present; and
past misdeeds demand atonement.

Although Fitzgerald and Faulkner have very differ
ent conceptions of time, they both depict, for differ
ent reasons, their heroes caught in a world of decay
and decline. To do this, they both extend the narra
tive limits of their novels, relate the plight of the hero
to the plight of society, and account for the plight of
society in terms of myth (Faulkner) or metaphysic
(Fitzgerald). In *The Great Gatsby*, for example
Fitzgerald relates Gatsby's lost dream to the loss of
the frontier and the American dream, which he in
turn relates to the metaphysical question of time
(" 'You can't repeat the past,' " says Nick Carraway)
In *Tender Is the Night*, Fitzgerald accounts on one
level for Dick's rise and fall, on another level for the
whole process of social decay in Western civilization
evident in the fate of the aristocratic class and the
plight of America after the Civil War and World
War I (suggested by reference to General U.S. Grant

urope's battle-field cemeteries, and the death of
ick's father who embodied the old virtues), and on a
nal level for Dick's fate in terms of man's hopeless
ght against time. In *Absalom, Absalom!,* Faulkner
lates the plight of Thomas Sutpen to the story of
ie Civil War (Henry Sutpen's killing Charles Bon is
kind of fratricide) and to the story of the Bible (the
se of the Absalom legend and of Sutpen's descent
om the Edenic world of the West Virginia moun-
ins to the tideland area of Virginia which is de-
ribed as a "fall" and which leads to the total loss of
utpen's innocence). In "The Bear," Faulkner relates
ie death of Sam Fathers and the bear to what
appened to the South after the Civil War when the
idustrialized North destroyed the old agrarian order
both Boon and the dog Lion, who kill the bear, are
nked by descriptive detail to the destructive ma-
iine: Lion is a "strange color like a blued-gun-
arrel," and Boon has a "blue stubble on his face like
ie filings from a new gun barrel"). Faulkner, in turn,
lates the death of the bear, again by descriptive
etail, to the rape of the forest by the lumber
ompany: "[The bear] fell all of a piece, as *a tree
lls*" [italics mine].[47] The death of the bear, the loss
f the Old South, the rape of the forest—all have one
use: the incest and miscegenation of Carothers
IcCaslin. Like Fitzgerald's novels, then, "The Bear"
inctions on three levels of reality—the level of the
idividual (the hunt); the level of history (the loss of
ie Old South), and the level of myth (the loss of the
ilderness, a kind of Eden).

While Faulkner and Fitzgerald extend their novels
i widening concentric circles, Faulkner's fiction is
ry different in both theme and tone from Fitzger-
d's. If in the center of Faulkner's novel is a sin that
ust be redeemed, in the center of Fitzgerald's is a
nse of promise, hope, and expectation. If Faulkner's
ero is preoccupied with the past, Fitzgerald's hero is
reoccupied with the future. If Faulkner's characters

IRONY AND THE THREE
REALMS OF TIME

ALTHOUGH Fitzgerald by temperament was Romantic, his best work was written out of his own sense of experience. He once remembered a time he was humiliated playing prep school football and how afterwards he wrote a poem for the school paper about his shame "which made me . . . a hit with my father." "So when I went home that Christmas vacation," he continued, "it was in my mind that if you weren't able to function in action you might at least be able to tell about it, because you felt the same intensity—it was a back door way out of facing reality." [1]

Fitzgerald always brought his personal experience to his best fiction, and he often wrote with a desire to relieve and to cope with his sense of hurt. When his imagination fixed upon men whom he admired, he would attempt to write their story, but it would inevitably become his own story. The final version would be more heightened and glamorous than he had experienced it; the hero, while often self-indulgent, was usually the victim of cruel and careless people. Fitzgerald depicted the idealist in conflict with the materialist, and conveyed his sense of loss at the hands of heartless people. He came to believe that these personal themes had their parallel in history; and he often extended meaning in his novels, through metaphor and allusion, until the story of his hero related to the story of America—the idealism of democracy in conflict with ruthless materialism, the pre-bellum years in contrast to the post-bellum, and the frontier in contrast to the modern world. Fitzger ald also depicted his idealistic hero trying to preserve a special moment of time—to arrest the days of youth and promise—and Fitzgerald sometimes extended his novels, like ripples spreading in a pond, beyond history to metaphysics—to man's tragic fight with the reality of time.

These larger themes, however, always had their source of origin in Fitzgerald's personal experience and he always wrote out of a deep sense of his own past. Critics often talk of Hemingway's wounding and his wounded hero. Fitzgerald also suffered a number of wounds. At an impressionistic age he lost a girl because he was not rich enough; the girl he finally married broke down mentally; dissipation and waste clotted his path; false starts and unrealized plans haunted him. He once wrote in his Notebook, "[I take] things hard—from Ginevra [King] to Joe Mank [Mankiewicz]," referring to the girl he lost in 1917 and to his disappointment twenty years later as a Hollywood writer. Such hurt, he said, is "the stamp that goes into my books so that people can read it blind like Braille." [2]

Fitzgerald's life—Princeton, Ginevra King, Zelda the Riviera, Hollywood—becomes the material for his fiction, and it is difficult to read his novels without placing them in a biographical context which in turn adds to them another dimension of meaning. Born on the doorstep of the twentieth century, coming to age during World War I, feeling himself so immediately a part of youth's postwar disillusionment, visiting the speakeasies during prohibition, meeting Arnold Roth stein who was the J. P. Morgan of the underworld enjoying the constant company of Ring Lardner who often played golf with Harding and who was a part of the dynamic life of New York in the twenties, living in France with such expatriates as Ernest Hemingway and Gerald Murphy, being the center of literary and social attention, drinking and partying and drinking—Fitzgerald's life perfectly paralleled the boom—and the bust. In 1930, Zelda had a mental breakdown; Fitzgerald's writing went slower; sickness and suffering surrounded him; his next novel was only mildly received; and he could not seem to get started again after its publication. Then came Hollywood. He had once again the hope of a new start, the old excitement and sense of new promise—only it all went flat. Fitzgerald knew that his experiences embodied the glamor of the wild twenties and pathetically suggested the dead-end conclusions of that life and the horror of the thirties. He tried to find visible forms—and he did not have to go very far outside of his own life—to objectify the spirit of his times. Fitzgerald was a spokesman, and he knew it.

When one calls Fitzgerald a spokesman for the young, one usually means that he wrote about young people—their activities, mannerisms, and fads. The statement, however, should mean much more, because Fitzgerald had a definite attitude toward youth that was basic to almost everything that he wrote. He came to think of youth as a fixed quantity of energy and vitality—a kind of emotional capital—to be invested with such care that it would pay the highest dividends. He believed, in other words, that youth was a time of promise—of expectation and possibility—a time to create the "platonic" image of what one wished to be. If one misspent and wasted these years given in trust, emotional bankruptcy followed.

The causes for such concern are difficult to isolate. Perhaps Fitzgerald put a premium on youth because of his own experience. At twenty-four he wrote a best-selling novel; at twenty-nine he published his most accomplished work, *The Great Gatsby*. He once wrote about this early success, "The man who arrives young believes that he exercises his will because his star is shining. . . . The compensation for a very early success is a conviction that life is a romantic matter." [3] Certainly life was a romantic matter for Fitzgerald, and he seems to have believed this even before *This Side of Paradise* was published. He idealized beautiful girls, football, Princeton, the career of the novelist; he even idealized war. Youth excited him, and he responded enthusiastically to it. "After all life hasn't much to offer except youth," he once wrote. [4] A time of hopeful longing, youth encouraged the dreams that eventually wilted with time. Youth is an "eternal morning of desire [which] passes to time and earthy afternoon." [5] These are the words of a boy twenty-one; but ten years later, writing about his last days at Princeton, the theme is exactly the same: "Some of us wept because we knew we'd never be quite so young any more as we had been here." [6]

Hemingway was right when he wrote Fitzgerald in December of 1935 that "You put so damned much value on youth"; Hemingway may also have been right when he continued, "it seems to me that you confused growing up with growing old." [7] The Hemingway hero often undergoes moral growth. Nick Adams and Lieutenant Henry, for example, become toughened and hardened by events, and their innocence gives way to experience. The Fitzgerald hero, however, with perhaps the exception of Nick Carraway, tries to sustain his youthful vision—his sense of expectancy—and thus he seems to remain innocent even in the face of experience.

For Fitzgerald, youth was fraught with the excitement of expectancy, the eternal hope of great accomplishment. "I should say," he wrote, "that, underneath the whole thing [his philosophy of life] lay a sense of infinite possibilities that was always with me whether vanity or shame was my mood." [8] Here we have, in Fitzgerald's words, the way he was to view youth: it brought with it *a sense of infinite possibilities*. "EVERYTHING IS POSSIBLE I AM IN

THE LAND OF AMBITION AND SUCCESS," he wired Zelda in February of 1919 upon reaching New York to take up work in the advertising business.[9]

This is Fitzgerald's idealized time—time as opportunity about to be realized, time as a germinating seed. This is the Keatsian element that runs through his fiction—the belief in a golden world, a beautiful moment that will never fade. Gatsby is destroyed because he cannot see that time does not operate this way—that the idealized moment cannot be sustained forever. Fitzgerald, like Gatsby, also tried to arrest time; and when this failed, when youth faded, he idealized the past and tried to relive it.

Perhaps Fitzgerald's clearest attitude toward the romantic past appears in his article "My Lost City." Here he describes what New York meant to him in his youth. But he is writing in 1932, the old feeling of excitement has vanished, and "seen from the ferry boat in the early morning, [New York] no longer whispers of fantastic success and eternal youth." Youth is gone, but Fitzgerald clearly reveals a fervent longing for the past. "For the moment," he concludes, "I can only cry out that I have lost my splendid mirage. Come back, come back, O glittering and white!" [10]

Here the Keatsian idealized time has given way to nostalgia; trust in the present is replaced by memory of the past. Both these attitudes toward time—the belief in an idealized moment, and the memory of a glamorized past—are present in *The Great Gatsby*. Gatsby idealizes the moment, and Nick Carraway nostalgically regrets that the moment has passed. When Nick realizes that Gatsby has lost Daisy and that the dream is dead, he remarks: "I just remembered that today's my birthday." I was thirty. . . . Thirty—the promise of a decade of loneliness . . . a thinning briefcase of enthusiasm, thinning hair." [11]

Thirty became for Fitzgerald the tragic age—the day of reckoning and of disillusionment—when the dream gave way to reality, and when one had to see himself not in terms of what might be but in terms of what was. This sense of regret for a faded world is the source of nostalgia in such novels and stories as *The Great Gatsby*, *Tender Is the Night*, "Winter Dreams," "The Last of the Belles," and "Babylon Revisited." As he grew older, Fitzgerald raised the age of reckoning a few years, but he continued to believe that life divided into two—that one looked forward to an idealized image of himself, and that later one looked backward to the glamor of older days. And yet escape into the romantic past could never be complete because the road back was too heavily lined with signs of waste and dissipation.

If Fitzgerald's attitude toward the past was ambivalent, so was his attitude toward money. He is said to have worshipped money, but this is not true. He saw money as a means, not an end—as a means to greater mobility, as a means to the heightened world that his imagination had created. And yet Fitzgerald distrusted the very rich and was suspicious of them. The reason for this stems from an experience that has not as yet been fully investigated. In January of 1917, Ginevra King, from a very wealthy Chicago family, broke with Fitzgerald, and on September 24, 1918 she married William Mitchell. Ginevra's father never approved of his daughter's interest in Scott. Charles King was a wealthy broker. He was born in 1873 into a prominent Chicago family of mortgage bankers. In 1894, when he left Yale, he joined the family firm of Shanklin and King, and in 1906 he organized his own firm—King, Farnum and Co. He kept two homes—in the winter living at 1450 Astor Street in Chicago, and in the summer on Ridge Road in Lake Forest. To Mr. King, Fitzgerald was from another world, and Fitzgerald soon became aware that he was considered socially beneath Ginevra. ("My father often gave him [Fitzgerald] a piece of his mind," Mrs. Marjorie King Belden, Ginevra's sister, told me.) If Fitzgerald had thought of himself as a poor boy in a rich man's world before, it was never to such a degree; but now that he had lost the girl whom he loved, he felt that his lack of money was the fault. Years later Fitzgerald was to advise his daughter to marry someone who follows a "calculated path stemming from a talent or money." [12] He could say this, and at the same time he could distrust the very rich, seeing them as careless and ruthless. His sense of hurt led him to this conclusion—led him, as I shall show later, to model Tom Buchanan on Charles King, Ginevra's father, and on William Mitchell, Ginevra's husband.

Fitzgerald's was the double view, and this is also true of his attitude toward success. If his early success helped sustain his belief in the promises and possibilities of life, it also made him aware of how far back he could fall. If one can trust a fictionalized account of Fitzgerald's life, then Budd Schulberg has said this when he suggested in *The Disenchanted* that Manley Halliday's success destroyed him—ruined a sense of self-discipline. Early success meant a lot to Fitzgerald, especially because he considered his father a failure. "You have to show up your own father." [13] Fitzgerald once wrote, and this is what Fitzgerald did when he became, after the publication of *This Side of Paradise*, a best selling novelist.

The money in Fitzgerald's family did not come from Fitzgerald's father—it came from Philip McQuillan, Fitzgerald's maternal grandfather who amassed by 1877 a fortune of $266,289.49 in the St. Paul wholesale and grocery business.[14] Mollie McQuillan, Fitzgerald's mother, married in February of 1890 Edward Fitzgerald who grew up on a Maryland farm, near Rockville in Montgomery County. He moved to St. Paul and, in the eighties, set up a modest wicker furniture business. In 1898 this business failed, and Edward Fitzgerald took his family to Buffalo, New York where he worked as a salesman for Procter and Gamble. In March of 1908, a day the eleven-year-old

Scott vividly remembered, Procter and Gamble fired his father. Almost thirty years later, four years before his own death, Fitzgerald spoke of that day with genuine feeling—and he thought of it in terms of lost youth and failure:

> "That morning he had gone out a comparatively young man, [Fitzgerald recalled in an interview] a man full of strength, full of confidence. He came home that evening an old man, a completely broken man. He had lost his essential drive, his immaculateness of purpose. He was a failure the rest of his days." [15]

This is a most revealing statement: Edward Fitzgerald, born in 1853, was fifty-five on the day he lost his job, and it is extraordinary how the man who once wrote "She was a faded but still lovely woman of twenty-seven" could at this time speak of his father as "a comparatively young man." Fitzgerald somehow had come to associate the idea of failure with his father—and with "lost youth"—and he seems to have held to this feeling throughout his life. What he said in this interview of 1936—two years after the publication of *Tender Is the Night*—differs little from what he said in June of 1926—a year after the publication of *The Great Gatsby*—when he wrote to Harold Ober, his agent, that "[my father's] own life after a brilliant start back in the seventies has been a 'failure' —he's lived always in mother's shadow and he takes an immense vicarious pleasure in any success of mine." [16] Like his father, Fitzgerald began his career with "a brilliant start," and he feared that his vitality would also run out. If one held on to youth interminably, he held on to the energy that made success possible. Belief in the magic vitality of youth led to the fear of passing thirty. Fitzgerald once told Maxwell Perkins that he wanted to die at thirty, [17] and in late September of 1928 he was disturbed enough to record in his Ledger, "Thirty-two years old and sore as hell about it." [18]

In the fiction that Fitzgerald wrote after thirty—for example, *Tender Is the Night* and "The Rough Crossing" (1929)—a beautiful *young* girl always appears and draws the aging hero back to a time of vitality and strength. When Adrian, of "The Rough Crossing," kisses Betsy D'Amido, "Her youth seemed to flow into him, bearing him up into a delicate romantic ecstasy that transcended passion. He couldn't relinquish it; he had discovered something that he thought was lost with his own youth forever." [19] Even Fitzgerald's most dissipated characters hate to admit that they have lost the vitality of youth. In "Financing Finnegan," Fitzgerald draws upon one of his own experiences and describes an "aging" writer who, in an attempt to recapture the spirit of his lost youth, breaks his shoulder diving from the highboard: " 'he saw some young girls diving from the fifteen-foot board. He says he thought of his lost youth and went up to do the same and made a beautiful swan dive—but his shoulder broke while he was still in the air.' " [20] In *Tender Is the Night,* Fitzgerald tried to show the extreme contrast between a vital and energetic Dick Diver who at the beginning of the novel is the emotional nucleus of the Riviera crowd, and a worn-out dissipated Diver who at the end of the novel is human flotsam. The pathos of Dick's condition, the contrast between the past and the present, is effectively portrayed in a water skiing episode when Dick humiliates himself trying to do a trick that ten years ago he could have handled with ease. In a Josephine story, "Emotional Bankruptcy," Fitzgerald makes it explicitly clear that such wasted youth is a moral matter. The heroine, after a riotous youth, suddenly finds that she can now "feel nothing at all." [21] This is a *Saturday Evening Post* sentiment, but Fitzgerald is not trying to market an idea that is suited to popular taste. When his daughter, Scottie, got into trouble at Ethel Walker's School—for hitchhiking to a New Haven dinner date—Fitzgerald wrote her that "For premature adventure one pays an atrocious price. . . . It's in the logic of life that no young person 'gets away with anything.' They fool their parents but not their contemporaries. It was in the cards that Ginevra King should get fired from Westover—also that your mother should wear out young." [22] "Our danger," he wrote Scottie a little later, "is imagining we have resources—material and moral —which we haven't got. . . . Do you know what bankruptcy exactly means? It means drawing on resources which one does not possess. . . . But I think that, like me, you will be something of a fool in that regard all your life, so I am wasting my words." [23]

One had only so much energy to spend before there was nothing left to draw upon. Fitzgerald, deeply concerned with how the energy was used, believed that carelessness accelerated the process of deterioration, and the waste in his own life haunted him. "I had been only a mediocre caretaker of most things left in my hands, even of my talent," [24] he said late in his life, repeating earlier words: "—Waste and horror— what I might have been and done that is lost, spent, gone, dissipated, unrecapturable. I could have acted thus, refrained from this, been bold where I was timid, cautious where I was rash." [25]

For all his fear of failure, Fitzgerald seemed to court it. If consciously he took pleasure in succeeding while his father had failed, perhaps (to refer to Freud) he feared to go beyond his father. Fitzgerald wasted money to the very edge of disaster. If this was in any way a rebellion against the staid life of his parents, it was also a form of willed destruction and perhaps a fear to go beyond them, a desire to fail so that he could show that they were really right. Certainly Fitzgerald punished himself by cruel drinking and by general dissipation; and he punished the artist in him by living beyond his means and forcing himself to do hack work for the popular magazines. The destructive quality in Dick Diver's character is also in Fitzgerald's. And strangely, while his father's failure haunted him, he was also haunted by his father's virtues—the virtues that Fitzgerald predicated of the pre-bellum South in general and of his father in particular. "My generation of radicals and breakers-down," Fitzgerald once wrote, "never found anything to take the place of the old virtues of work and courage and the old graces of courtesy and politeness." [26] These were the virtues that Dick Diver's father so well embodied. Fitzgerald, unlike Dreiser, could never write a novel that implied the wages of sin might be success. The man of self-discipline in him harked back to the old-fashioned morality of his upbringing; the man of self-indulgence was a somewhat manufactured product of the adolescent mind bent on random revolt from parental authority and copybook clichés.

The feud within—the man of self-discipline at war with the man of self-indulgence—led to Fitzgerald's ambivalent attitude toward the past. It is this ambivalence—nostalgia for lost glamor, guilt about the waste of possibilities—that Wright Morris fails to see. Morris points out that the past for Fitzgerald became a glamorous limbo, "where the artist could graze like a horse put to pasture, feeding on such clover . . . as whets the appetite." [27] He fails, however, to point out that the past also held horror. As Fitzgerald put it in 1931, "Now once more the belt is tight and we summon the proper expression of horror as we look back at our wasted youth." [28]

If the idealized moment often gives way to nostalgia in Fitzgerald's fiction, nostalgia in turn often gives way to the horror of wasted youth, and it is within these three realms of time—time idealized, time sentimentalized, and time regretted—that Fitzgerald's fiction works.

In "Echoes of the Jazz Age," Fitzgerald tells us that the Jazz Age "began about the time of the May Day riots in 1919, and leaped to a spectacular death in October, 1929." [29] He had believed all along that thirty was the tragic age and that emotional bankruptcy resulted from misinvested energy. What seemed true in terms of his own experience now seemed true in terms of history. "Babylon Revisited"—a story where the horror of the past prevails—suggests that the depression was an ultimate consequence of misspent vitality, and reveals the way Fitzgerald connected the personal and the public tragedy.

As he felt the relationship between the depression and his lost youth, Fitzgerald also believed that the frontier embodied the youth of America, a time of great possibility, the beginning "of all aspiration." He worked this idea into *The Great Gatsby*, and he seemed intent on getting it into *The Last Tycoon*. Fitzgerald identified the American dream with "the human dream and if I came at the end of it," he said, "that too is a place in the line of the pioneers." [30] Monroe Stahr comes at the end of the dream, and *The Last Tycoon* looks nostalgically back to a pristine and vital time, to "younger" days in the movie industry and to "younger" days in America.

The premium that Fitzgerald put on youth and the promises of life was both an asset and a handicap to his fiction. If there is a little bit of the romantic in each of us, to act and write accordingly leads to overstatement and sentimentality. This is certainly what happened in *This Side of Paradise*, a hopeless novel by any standards. Fitzgerald must have known this when he came to *The Beautiful and Damned*—a novel in which life dominates the characters instead of their dominating life; a novel of frustration and deterioration akin in idea to the essays of H. L. Mencken, Harold Frederic's *The Damnation of Theron Ware*, and Theodore Dreiser's *Sister Carrie*. This is Fitzgerald's first experience with irony; but it is a naturalistic irony, an irony of situation, where the hope and expectations of Anthony and Gloria Patch are continually thwarted. The novel suffers from an imperfect reconciliation between Fitzgerald's sense of experience and the literary means of expressing it. In fact, the sense of life in *The Beautiful and Damned* does not really emerge from Fitzgerald's own experience, just as the ending of *This Side of Paradise* does not either. The disillusionment in *The Beautiful and Damned* was not Fitzgerald's own, and he is writing at cross currents with himself. His interest was never in the meaning or the meaninglessness of life (he took for granted that it had meaning), but in the promise of life in confrontation with the destructive element, the inexorable workings of time. To this theme Fitzgerald's imagination could warm; and while this element is an important one in *The Beautiful and Damned*, the full significance of it becomes confused with the pseudo theme of the meaning and the meaninglessness of life. When Fitzgerald began writing *The Great Gatsby*, he stripped away what was false to his experience and wrote out of a spirit of conviction. He created a heightened world, opened the door, and slipped in—bringing with him his own boyhood dreams of becoming like James J. Hill (the Dan Cody of the novel) and his resentment over losing Ginevra King and almost losing Zelda Sayre (who combined are Daisy Fay). What Fitzgerald also brings to this novel is the ironic mode—not naturalistic irony—but rhetorical, a double voice: Gatsby's idealistic voice and Nick Carraway's somewhat cynical one. The double voice lends itself to the double vision —the ability of Fitzgerald to see himself in Gatsby as both "gorgeous" and "meretricious," as both admirable and vulgar. When it came to depicting the Buchanans in double focus, the imagination faltered because the King family was too much in mind, the wound was still open, bleeding like that of the haemophile, to use Fitzgerald's own metaphor.[31]

In *The Great Gatsby*, Fitzgerald created a situation where the dream floundered upon the rocks of the very rich, and he found a way of controlling the overstatement of excited youth by describing the dreamer

IN NOVEMBER of 1939, Fitzgerald wrote to a Miss
Kent, who had just sent him a manuscript: "You have
an idea—but scarcely a story, do you think? . . . I
don't think there's enough here to hold the reader's
attention . . . lacking [is] . . . a point of real interest, a true climax rather than a succession of incidents
which do not build to an instant of real excitement." [1]
These words well describe Fitzgerald's own *This Side
of Paradise*, at least for us today, some forty-five years
after it was written.

Fitzgerald seems to have an idea but scarcely a
story; there is not enough to hold the reader's attention; the novel does not build to a true climax; and the
plot is trite: Amory Blaine goes to a prep school and
then Princeton, flunks geometry and loses his place on
the *Princetonian* and a possible seat on the Senior
Council, is shocked by Dick Humbird's accidental
death, falls in love four times, sees the ghost of Dick
Humbird, goes into the army, works briefly in advertising, accepts the blame for Alec Connage's illicit affair,
and visits Princeton to brood over the ashes of his
youth.

Amory is in love with the image of himself in love,
and his unrequited love is at best melodramatic. He
thinks that he and his friends are profound when their
ideas are commonplace and superficial. Fitzgerald
overstates their attitude toward each other, and toward life, and the novel is hopelessly sentimental.

ROSALIND [*Commencing to sob again*] It's been so
    perfect—you and I. So like a dream that I'd longed
    for and never thought I'd find. The first real unself-
    ishness I've ever felt in my life. And I can't see it
    fade out in a colorless atmosphere!
AMORY It won't—it won't!
ROSALIND I'd rather keep it as a beautiful memory—
    tucked away in my heart. [2]

Rosalind, one of the flappers Fitzgerald made famous, seems uninteresting now, but we all know how
she fascinated Fitzgerald and the large audience that
bought his first novel. Amory admired the flapper,
although his Puritanism was shocked by her haughty
freedom and exciting recklessness. He saw her "doing
things that even in his memory would have been
impossible: eating three-o'clock, after-dance suppers
in impossible cafés, talking of every side of life with an
air half of earnestness, half of mockery, yet with a
furtive excitement that Amory considered stood for a
real moral letdown. But he never realized how wide-
spread it was until he saw the cities between New
York and Chicago as one vast juvenile intrigue"
[59].

Fitzgerald can state Amory's feelings, but he cannot
convincingly dramatize them; and while the novel was
read as a statement of the new morality, it is really
much more a sentimental story about youth's attempt
to commit itself in a changing world.

Fitzgerald was obsessed with three events in his life
when he was writing *This Side of Paradise:* his failure
to win the loves of Ginevra King and Zelda Sayre; his
failure to get a Princeton degree; and his romantic
fascination with the perils of war.

Fitzgerald rehearsed his hurt over losing Ginevra
King in his early writing. The apprentice pieces
"Babes in the Woods" and "The Debutante" depict
this romance—first the young love and the petting
parties, then the cool dismissal. Both these pieces were
used in *This Side of Paradise*—Isabelle Borgé (Gi-

nevra King) is the Isabelle of "Babe in the Woods."
What is of interest is that Rosalind (Zelda Sayre) in
This Side of Paradise is substituted for Helen Halycon
in "The Debutante" who was originally modelled on
Ginevra.[3] Fitzgerald fused the experience he had with
Ginevra and Zelda, welding his hurt over losing
Ginevra with his hurt over losing Zelda who did not
marry him until after *This Side of Paradise* was pub-
lished.

In fact, in *This Side of Paradise*, Fitzgerald moved
from a description of Isabelle (Ginevra King) to
Rosalind (Ginevra and Zelda) to Eleanor (Zelda
Sayre). A process of metamorphosis is at work here,
Fitzgerald moving from one character, to a composite
character, to a third character who was contained in
the second. We know from the biographies the many
eccentricities of Zelda Sayre, especially her tendency
toward self-destruction. One night in Paris, for example, she threw herself headlong down a flight of
stairs.[4] In Rosalind, this takes the form of daredevil
recklessness and a competitiveness with men. She
dives "from the top of a rickety, thirty-foot summer-
house" [189] and she is slightly disgusted when Harvard Gillespie, forced by pride to follow, "stooped"
when he dove. With Eleanor, this recklessness becomes more self-destructive. The same night that she
confesses to Amory that her mother "went mad—
stark raving crazy," she rides her horse toward a cliff,
falling off ten feet before the horse plunges over [cf.
239–40].

In *This Side of Paradise*, Fitzgerald fused and
combined many disparate elements of his experience.
His imagination would continue to function in this
way throughout his career, and in *The Great Gatsby*,
as I shall show, he again fused Ginevra and Zelda in
the character of Daisy Fay.

Fitzgerald first expressed the resentment he felt
about his failure to pass his Princeton academic work
in "The Spire and the Gargoyle," published in the

February 1917 edition of *Nassau Literary Magazine.*
The spires, of course, are part of the Gothic Princeton
architecture; the gargoyle is the young preceptor who
proctored, graded, and failed the young hero on his
first final exam, causing him to be dismissed from the
university. In New York, the hero later meets the
young instructor, who has left Princeton to teach in a
Brooklyn high school. When the young man returns
to Princeton for a sentimental visit, he meets the
instructor on the train. When they arrive on campus,
the hero cannot go on, goes instead back to the train,
where he "cried out from a complete overwhelming
sense of failure" [114].

In *This Side of Paradise,* Fitzgerald preserved the
dynamics of this story: Princeton remains the romantic setting—Gothic buildings bathed in moonlight;
the administration becomes the gargoyle; and the
young hero continues to feel self-pity. The trouble
with Fitzgerald's handling of the Princeton experience
is the same trouble he had with handling his love
affairs: he is unable to assimilate the experience
dramatically, to find an objective correlative to convey
his feeling, and the novel is distorted by Amory's self-
pity.

War does not play a major part in *This Side of
Paradise.* Fitzgerald reveals that Amory goes to war in
a section called "Interlude," in which Amory, at a
port of embarkation, receives a letter from Monsignor
Darcy. This is followed by one of Fitzgerald's poems
entitled "Embarking at Night." Finally, there is a
letter from Amory to Tom D'Invilliers [modelled on
John Peale Bishop], expressing Amory's disillusionment with war, American politics, religion, and life,
and asking D'Invilliers to share a Manhattan apartment with him.

Fitzgerald is fighting his own emotions when he
expresses Amory's disillusionment in war and life. In
an early short story—"Sentiment—and the Use of
Rouge," published in June of 1917 in *Nassau Literary*

Magazine—a young British lieutenant comes home on leave after two years at war to find everything changed: his sister wears too much "paint," and Eleanor (who was engaged to his brother, killed in battle) tells him that women are morally relaxed because "we can't be [your wives]—therefore we'll be as much as we can" [154]. When he returns to battle, the young man is shot and dies thinking that "everything [is] a muddle, everybody offside, and the referee gotten rid of" [159].

The puritan shock at relaxed morals is Fitzgerald's, but the sense of disillusionment—the feeling of meaninglessness—is not. Fitzgerald wanted more than anything else at this time in his life to get overseas; the war was part of the heroic mode, along with football, and he remained true to this rather extraordinary view his whole life.[5] The feelings of disillusionment in this fiction are thus not his; they are instead the clichés of the smart set.

While much of Fitzgerald's own personal experience is rendered unconvincing in *This Side of Paradise*, the expression of postwar despair is even less convincing because it is the least sincere. In his later fiction, Fitzgerald would make use of his genuine belief in the promise and possibility of life, and he would counterpoint this heightened view against opposed states of mind and emotion, creating an ironic complexity. There is no such complexity in *This Side of Paradise*, and the fault with the novel is that the emotions of his characters are not controlled—they are heightened to the point of outrageous sentimentality or they are cynical to the point of pretension.

In *This Side of Paradise*, Fitzgerald was unable to assimilate his emotions convincingly. The reasons for this is that Fitzgerald's novel is really very derivative, and the limitations of *This Side of Paradise* are, in part, the limitations of Compton Mackenzie's *Sinister Street*. The similarities of plot between the two novels are obvious: Mrs. Fane and Mrs. Blaine are both well-bred and comically superficial; both Michael Fane and Amory grow up without a father; Michael turns as a substitute for his father to the Reverend Mr. Viner and Amory turns to Monsignor Darcy; Michael goes to Oxford, Amory goes to Princeton, and they both become disillusioned with war and country; the conversations between Michael and Aunt Maud are at times strangely similar to the conversations between Amory and Cousin Clara; both Michael and Amory move back and forth between feelings of intensity and feelings of emptiness; both Michael and Amory are vaguely concerned with the problems of evil (cf. Michael's sense of responsibility for Lily with Amory's fascination for Eleanor); and Michael at the end converts to Catholicism while Amory at the end thinks seriously of Catholicism before he rejects it "for the present." Both Michael and Amory, conventional and at times even prudish, romanticize and idealize life, feign (or should it be Fane?) a tragic attitude, and each novel bogs down in sentiment and mooncalf emotion. "He must have Lily," writes Mackenzie. "How damnable were these silver nights of June, how their fragrance musk-like even here in London fretted him with the imagination of wasted beauty." [6] "All the way back [Eleanor] talked haltingly about herself, and Amory's love waned slowly with the moon," Fitzgerald writes. "The stars were long gone and there were left only the little sighing gust of wind and the silences between" [240]. The tone of *Sinister Street* becomes a serious liability in *This Side of Paradise* and even *The Beautiful and Damned*, a liability Fitzgerald does not overcome until he learns in *The Great Gatsby* to establish a greater distance between his main characters and their romantic emotions.

Perhaps the most important point of comparison between *Sinister Street* and *This Side of Paradise* is the attitude that both Mackenzie and Fitzgerald take toward youth. Like Amory, "Michael only demanded the courage not to waste youth while it was his to enjoy" [317], and he goes in search of new experience expecting each adventure to unlock the mysteries of life. What Michael discovers is that such a quest is useless, that it leads to continued disillusionment, and that it stems from the false idealism of youth. Michael Fane finally arrives at a kind of peace; he looks forward to the future; he only regrets that he spent so much time on what now seems "the pettiness of youthful tragedies." This is the way *Sinister Street* ends:

> "All that I have done and experienced so far," Michael thought, "would not scratch this stone. I have been concerned for the happiness of other people without gratitude for the privilege of service. I have been given knowledge and I fancied I was given disillusion. . . . Rome! Rome! how parochial you make my youth." [879–80]

The situation is completely different in *This Side of Paradise*. Amory does not think of youth as only an avenue to maturity. He does not question the idealism of youth—only the ideals; and he feels that he sacrificed his youth to dead gods, to the false ideals of the past. Unlike Michael Fane, Amory Blaine finds no peace, looks forward to no future, and his youthful tragedies do not seem insignificant or petty. This is the way *This Side of Paradise* ends:

> There was no God in his heart, he knew; his ideas were still in riot; there was ever the pain of memory; the regret for his lost youth—yet the water of disillusion had left a deposit on his soul, responsibility and a love of life, the faint stirring of old ambitions and unrealized dreams. But—oh, Rosalind! Rosalind! [282]

An examination of *bildungsroman* fiction written approximately at the time of *This Side of Paradise* reveals that Fitzgerald handled his theme of youth as something very personal and not as a matter of convention. In fact, if there is a conventional way of looking at youth, it is Compton Mackenzie's view that maturity begins when the fires of youth recede. Compare, for example, Stephen Vincent Benét's *The Beginning of Wisdom*: "He [Philip Sellaby] saw where often he had mistaken the mere hardness and shelliness of youth for strength and its bluster for logic. . . ."[7] Also Floyd Dell's *The Briary-Bush*:

> *Oh, the briary-bush,*
> *That pricks my heart so sore!*
> *If I ever get out of the briary-bush*
> *I'll never get in any more![8]*

The "briary-bush" is, of course, the urges of youth. Compare, finally, John Dos Passos' *Streets of Night* in which the hero says that " 'Sentimentality about youth is the cheapest of all sentimentalities.' "[9]

This Side of Paradise is a novel about youth lost to misplaced ideals, which explains why, from the moment we first see him, Amory Blaine puzzles about what he wants to be. He has a romantic conception of himself—a sense of his own immense possibilities—that goes with Fitzgerald's concept of youth: "Amory wondered how people could fail to notice that he was a boy marked for glory. . . . Amory marked himself a fortunate youth, capable of infinite expansion for good or evil" [17–18].

Amory wants one experience to build on the next so that his life will have a sense of continuity. This makes him, according to Monsignor Darcy, a personage—not a personality. One must look ahead and see what he can be, and then life becomes "possibility" as he moves toward the goal. The personage is the youth buoyed up by a sense of purpose; the personality, on the other hand, is the youth who floats like a wind-drift balloon. The personality draws upon the energy of youth indiscriminately; the personage draws upon the energy of youth with a sense of mission.

And a sense of mission depends upon the power of imagination. One has to have an image of himself—

he must shine in the light of his own imagination—
and then work to realize the image. The image can
betray, but without it life becomes colorless. Fitzgerald drives this idea home in a conversation between
Amory and Burne Holiday as they walk one night in
the woods just off the campus. Burne tells Amory that
he often walks this alone and that he used to be afraid
because "'I peopled the woods with everything
ghastly.'" Burne then tells Amory that he eventually
controlled his fear by projecting his imagination
ahead of himself: [I] saw myself coming along the
road. That made it all right—as it makes everything
all right to project yourself completely into another's
place" [130].

This is an important passage because the idea here
becomes a cornerstone for Fitzgerald's narrative
method and fiction. Fitzgerald was continually projecting himself into other places and into other people. He was able to escape to a splendid realm on the
wings of imagination. The imagination became the
destructive faculty when, as in Gatsby's case, it prolonged the dream after time had run out. Amory's
cousin, Clara Page, a young widow with whom Amory
falls in love, tells him that he could easily become the
victim of his imagination: "You're a slave, a bound
helpless slave to one thing in the world, your imagination!" [143].

Unlike Gatsby, however, Amory does not become a
victim of his imagination—in fact, his imagination
saves him—or at least so Fitzgerald suggests. Amory
has his disappointments at Princeton, but he never
gives up his dream of succeeding at his writing for the
Princetonian and the Triangle Club. As slight as these
tasks may be, Amory uses them to create an image of
himself, and they give him a sense of purpose. As
Fitzgerald puts it: "The sense of going forward in a
direct, determined line had come back; youth was
stirring and shaking out a few new feathers" [136].
When these tasks become meaningless so does

Amory's life—and youth—and this is the note on which the novel closes.

The trouble with the ending of *This Side of Paradise* is that Fitzgerald tries to heighten his theme by suggesting that Amory squandered his youth when he miscommitted it to the old social and political ideals. The conversation at the end between Amory and Mr. Ferrenby grows out of nothing that comes before it, because Amory hitherto has had little interest in socialistic theories of war and poverty. Amory's sudden interest in weightier matters is an attempt to make his sense of commitment more significant, and hence the theme of wasted youth more tragic. We are supposed to believe that Amory is a victim of misguided commitment and to understand why, in his final visit to Princeton, he despairs over the others who will also be victimized by these creeds:

> Long after midnight the towers and spires of Princeton were visible, with here and there a late-burning light—and suddenly out of the clear darkness the sound of bells. As an endless dream it went on; the spirit of the past brooding over a new generation, the chosen youth from the muddled, unchastened world, still fed romantically on the mistakes and half-forgotten dreams of dead statesmen and poets. Here was a new generation, shouting the old cries, learning the old creeds, through a revery of long days and nights; destined finally to go out into that dirty gray turmoil to follow love and pride; a new generation dedicated more than the last to the fear of poverty and the worship of success; grown up to find all Gods dead, all wars fought, all faiths in man shaken. [282]

Examined within the novel's own terms, all this seems a little ridiculous. If Amory is betrayed by anything, it is the goddess of love and the administration at Princeton, which required him to take geometry and then, when he failed it, fired him from the *Princetonian*. Fitzgerald reveals that his own sense of "disillusionment" in college did not go far beyond a disillusionment with academic requirements. In a

letter defending *This Side of Paradise* to President
John Grier Hibben of Princeton, he said: "It was a
book written with the bitterness of my discovery that
I had spent several years trying to fit in with a
curriculum that is after all made for the average
student. After the curriculum had tied me up, taken
away the honors I'd wanted, bent my nose over a
chemistry book and said 'No fun, no activities, no
offices, no Triangle trips—no, not even a diploma if
you can't do chemistry'—after that I retired." [10]

Amory's long talk about the old creeds is a mere
device to give *This Side of Paradise* a thematic
importance it would not have otherwise. Edmund
Wilson gives Fitzgerald too much credit when he says
that intellectually *This Side of Paradise* "amounts to
little more than a gesture—a gesture of indefinite
revolt." [11] The objects of Amory's revolt are not
indefinite—they are inconsequential—and James E.
Miller, Jr. does not really clarify the matter when he
says that "the novel is more a representation of . . .
restlessness than it is a coherent assertion of revolt . . . what is being revolted *against* does not
clearly emerge." [12] The trouble with the novel is that
the objects of Amory's revolt *do* clearly emerge—but
they are sophomoric—and Amory's sense of youth
wasted by false commitment is more melodramatic
than tragic. Yet everything in the novel builds toward
this sense of waste, and the reader is meant to take the
following passages with high seriousness:

> Tireless passion, fierce jealousy, longing to possess and
> crush—these alone were left of all his love for Rosalind;
> *these remained to him as payment for the loss of his
> youth*—bitter calomel under the thin sugar of love's
> exaltation. [245, italics mine]

and

> There was no God in his heart, he knew; his ideas were
> still in riot; there was ever the pain of memory; *the
> regret for his lost youth*. [282, italics mine]

The last sentence gives us the key to the novel. It may be difficult to take Amory as seriously as he takes himself, and Fitzgerald may ask the reader to respond more emotionally than the situation deserves. The theme of the novel may be inadequately dramatized, but it is not as vague as the critical commentary suggests. Amory has paid for his "knowledge" with his youth, and for Fitzgerald it was a bitter price, " 'All a poor substitute at best,' " as Amory puts it.

This Side of Paradise is both a novel of youthful disappointment and disillusionment, and of youthful longing and hope. The sense of promise and the sense of loss, the capacity of wonder and the belief that life is a cheat, these feelings exist side by side in this novel, compete with one another, become contradictory, and tear the novel in two. Fitzgerald is unable to make dramatic use of Amory's states of mind, and Amory moves back and forth between contradictory positions in a world that does not exist.

There is no sense of place in *This Side of Paradise*. There is a heightened sense of feeling—the mood of youth under moonlight—but not the descriptive detail to anchor this feeling and make it real and convincing. Fitzgerald learned how to find an objective correlative for emotion in *The Great Gatsby*, and it is perhaps for this reason that the critics have not hitherto seen that *The Great Gatsby* has almost all of the elements of *This Side of Paradise*.

The themes in *This Side of Paradise* that stayed with Fitzgerald are those of the power of the imagination, the possibilities of youth, the tragedy of misguided commitment, and the destructive nature of time. Even the last page of *This Side of Paradise*—the discussion of the past rolling over the present—parallels in idea and phrasing the last page of *The Great Gatsby*. Earlier in *This Side of Paradise*, Tom says to Amory, " 'You know . . . what we feel now is the sense of the gorgeous youth that has rioted through here [Princeton] in two hundred years. . . . And what we leave here is more than this class; it's the whole heritage of youth' " [153]. Gatsby, to be sure, is not so formally a part of his generation as is Amory; despite his "Oxford days" he is not a part of any graduating class or any fixed social group. Gatsby's tragedy stems from his trying to buy back the fruits of youth, from his belief that five years have made no difference in his relationship with Daisy. The five years, of course, have made all the difference.

No one to my knowledge has noted the similarity of details between Michael and Lily in *Sinister Street* and Gatsby and Daisy in *The Great Gatsby*. The names (Lily and Daisy) are similar; both Lily and Daisy are seventeen when Michael and Gatsby first fall in love with them; and, like Gatsby, Michael Fane, separated from Lily for almost six years, is still in love with his memory of her. Before he again meets her, Mackenzie writes: "September became October. It would be six years this month since first they met, and she was twenty-two now. Could seventeen be captured anew?" [736]

Daisy gave her youth to Tom Buchanan, and the Daisy that Gatsby tries to win back is a changed woman—hardened and grown morally callous. Amory will have no such illusions about an older Rosalind; he tells us that he will not try to buy back time; and what Amory knows, Gatsby to his eventual sorrow, never learns:

> Never again could [Amory] find even the sombre luxury of wanting her—not this Rosalind, harder, older—nor any beaten, broken woman that his imagination brought to the door of his forties—Amory had wanted her youth, the fresh radiance of her mind and body, the stuff that she was selling now once and for all. So far as he was concerned, young Rosalind was dead. [253]

Although Amory and Gatsby end with different states of mind, the germ of *The Great Gatsby* is in *This Side of Paradise*. Both novels are about spent and misspent youth, about the loss of possibility and the end of expectation, and about the regret and pain of such loss—and both put the emphasis on the desire to relive the past:

> [I thought, says Amory, that] I regretted my lost youth when I only envy the delight of losing it. Youth is like having a big plate of candy. Sentimentalists think they want to be in the pure, simple state they were in before they ate the candy. They don't. They just want the fun of eating it all over again. The matron doesn't want to repeat her girlhood—she wants to repeat her honeymoon. I don't want to repeat my innocence. I want the pleasure of losing it again. [258]

This Side of Paradise is a very immature novel, but in many ways Fitzgerald rewrote it again and again. What he had to learn was to find the descriptive detail, the objective correlatives, to sustain the heightened world of infinite possibility. New York seen from the Queensboro Bridge, the view of the green light on Daisy's dock across the bay, the long sweep of velvet grass from water edge to the Buchanan mansion at East Egg, the terrible pink suits of Jay Gatsby—these details, and many more, would anchor the gorgeous world of Jay Gatsby to reality.

Fitzgerald had to learn, that is, to control his Keatsian view—his belief in a resplendent moment in conflict with time. He did this in *The Great Gatsby* by contrasting the romantic disposition of Gatsby with the less romantic mind of Nick Carraway and with the totally unromantic mind of the Buchanans.

Another way of saying this is that Fitzgerald had to reconcile the form of the romance with the form of the novel. Gatsby may embody the spirit of the frontier in a mythic way—he may be slightly larger than life; but he lives in a world of intricate social relationship—a world that is also physically alive. Fitzgerald in *The Great Gatsby* let his imagination,

ike a balloon, take flight; but a rope grounded it to a
pecific place at a specific moment of time, and the
mreal quality of a mysterious Jay Gatsby is grotes-
quely brought to earth by the totally real quality of
Tom Buchanan's Long Island. It is because of this
ack of place, this lack of grotesque contrast, this lack
of irony, that *This Side of Paradise* becomes unconvincing—misty in atmosphere and overstated in situa-
ion.

4 THE BEAUTIFUL AND DAMNED

The Beautiful and Damned picks up the thread o
This Side of Paradise. At the end of Fitzgerald's firs
novel, Amory has left Princeton, abandoned what w
are vaguely told are the meaningless creeds of the past
and is trying to find something to which he car
commit himself. Edmund Wilson has said that i
This Side of Paradise Fitzgerald "supposed that th
thing to do was to discover a meaning in life." [1] An
yet Amory's dislike of capitalism and his sympathy fo
socialism—all of which is merely appended to th
novel—seems to be the vaguest kind of commitmen
and when we last see him, he is still uprooted, lookin
at an uncertain future. If Fitzgerald wrote *This Sid
of Paradise* out of his Princeton experience, he wrot
The Beautiful and Damned out of his army an
postwar experience.

It has been assumed that Gloria Gilbert is modelle
completely on Zelda, but a closer look at the nove
reveals that Gloria, like Rosalind in *This Side o
Paradise*, really has two personalities, and again Fitz
gerald seems to be describing both Ginevra King an
Zelda Sayre. Ginevra King surrounded herself con
stantly with three friends, classmates at Westover
Edith Cummings (who becomes the model for Jorda
Baker in *The Great Gatsby*), Courtney Letts, an
Peggy Carry. They were all from Lake Forest, jus
outside of Chicago; all wore wedding rings for the fu

f it; and all made the rounds of the cafés when they
ame into New York from Westover. Gloria Gilbert
rrounds herself with two friends, classmates at
armover: Muriel Kane and Rachel Jerryl. They are
irts (Fitzgerald called Ginevra and her group
speeds"), and they also know their way around New
ork after dark.

"Once I thought that Lake Forest was the most
lamorous place in the world," Fitzgerald wrote near
he end of his life. And then he added, "Maybe it
as." [2] In The Beautiful and Damned, Fitzgerald
eems to be describing his own experience with Gi-
evra King and her family, who were from Lake Forest.
He depicts Gloria's father as unfavorably as Fitzgerald
hought of Mr. King. When Anthony first meets Mr.
Gilbert, "the young man and the old touched flesh;
Mr. Gilbert's hand was soft, worn away to the pulpy
emblance of a squeezed grapefruit." [3] Later Gloria's
ather is described as a bully of the soul [cf. 190].

The father disappears from the novel once Gloria
nd Anthony are married, but Joseph Bloeckman,
Anthony's fiercest competitor in love, does not. Fitz-
erald attended Ginevra King's wedding in 1918 when
he married William Mitchell who was in the banking
usiness and who was also a friend of Charles King, a
roker. It is interesting that Joseph Bloeckman should
e in the movie business and a close friend of Mr.
Gilbert, who has made his money in the related
elluloid industry. Fitzgerald, however, gave Anthony
he promise of fantastic money (Adam Patch is
riginally worth seventy-five million) and the advan-
age of an established family—exactly the way that
Fitzgerald would have liked to present himself to the
King family. Fitzgerald also made Anthony's competi-
or vulgar and socially unacceptable, and this is again
he way Fitzgerald would have liked it to be in his
wn life. Once again we see Fitzgerald using his
iction as a kind of escape, a form of daydream.

There are two Gloria Gilberts in The Beautiful and

Damned. One is the *femme fatale* who cruelly tease
Anthony. Fitzgerald, with Keats's "La Belle Dam
Sans Merci" in mind, tells a fantasy story in *Th
Beautiful and Damned* about a young knight wh
enters a monastery; takes the vows of poverty, cha
tity, obedience, and silence; and then is tempted to hi
death by the sight of a beautiful girl [cf. 89–92
Courting Zelda was difficult for Fitzgerald, but he di
after all win her, and the story of the girl withou
mercy—the girl who is indifferent to Anthony becaus
she is in love with a wealthier man—resembles Fitz
gerald's experience with Ginevra King.

The other Gloria Gilbert in *The Beautiful an
Damned* is the slightly schizophrenic girl who move
between states of exaggerated excitement and melan
choly pouting [cf. 111–12]. Although Fitzgerald onc
wrote that he and Zelda had a better time tha
Anthony and Gloria,[4] the woman Anthony marrie
seems very much like Zelda. Like the Fitzgeralds, th
Patches honeymoon in Santa Barbara. Also, like th
Fitzgeralds, their relationship is abrasive from th
beginning. Fitzgerald described Gloria as a "girl o
tremendous nervous tension and of the most high
handed selfishness" [157]. Gloria is egocentric, pleas
ure seeking, wild, impractical, and careless. She i
primarily concerned with getting her legs tanned
spends money with reckless abandon, is unpredictabl
and slightly suicidal (as, for example, the night sh
bolts toward an oncoming train when she become
dissatisfied with a drinking party), and she drives lik
a maniac.

If Fitzgerald is using *The Beautiful and Damned* a
a kind of daydream, achieving through his imagina
tion what he could not realize in life, he is also usin
this novel as a catharsis, depicting Gloria in a way tha
satisfied Fitzgerald emotionally—as a kind of vam
whose demands upon Anthony are excessive an
debilitating.

Although Fitzgerald is using his second novel fo

ome of the same emotional purposes as he used his
rst, *The Beautiful and Damned* marks an an advance
ver *This Side of Paradise*. Fitzgerald is developing a
ense of irony, of self-mockery. Dick Caramel remarks,
Everywhere I go some silly girl asks me if I've read
his Side of Paradise. If it is true to life, which I don't
elieve, the next generation is going to the dogs"
421]. Anthony feels superior to Dick at this point; he
elt a touch of the old pleasant contempt for his
riend" [423]. Yet Dick Caramel is another side of
itzgerald himself—and Dick and Anthony are in a
ay a bifurcation of their creator. Anthony exper-
nces Fitzgerald's loves. Caramel is the novelist with
n intense sense of purpose, who has written one suc-
essful book but who is wasting his time writing popu-
r trash for quick money. Fitzgerald had the ability
o project himself into the future—with a sense of
ope and also with a sense of uncertainty. Dick
aramel personifies the horror of what Fitzgerald felt
might happen to him—just as many years later Pat
lobby embodies Fitzgerald's fear of what he might
ecome. Caramel is the dedicated writer who has
asted his talent.

Besides a sense of irony, Fitzgerald is also develop-
ng in *The Beautiful and Damned* a sense of place. If
his Side of Paradise has no real sense of place, *The
Beautiful and Damned* is bedrocked in physical detail.
Anthony, for example, when we first see him, has a
pacious apartment with high ceilings in a brownstone
ouse on Fifty-second Street. He loves to walk along
ifth Avenue on a busy, crisp November day, and he
eels the sense of tension in the city, the "suppressed
xcitement." He likes to have a drink at the Plaza
lotel where, when we first meet her, Gloria Gilbert
ives with her family. New York in these scenes comes
live in *The Beautiful and Damned*.

When Fitzgerald further develops his craft—when
e knows better how to use irony based on a bifurca-
ion of conflicting emotion, and when he knows how

to use descriptive detail to make a world convincing—he will be able to write *The Great Gatsby,* his finest novel.

The Beautiful and Damned, as it stands, is a long way from *The Great Gatsby.* If *This Side of Paradise* is a novel of unassimilated emotion, *The Beautiful and Damned* is a novel of unassimilated idea. The theme of life's meaninglessness goes against the grain of Fitzgerald's conviction in the promises of life and the horror of wasted time and beauty. As Fitzgerald put it, "there was always, first of all, the sense of waste, always dormant in his [Anthony's] heart" [284]. Fitzgerald buried these real convictions under a pseudo theme.

Anthony Patch, like Amory Blaine, is supposed to be intellectually deracinated. Although well-educated, witty, intelligent, and handsome, he is completely uncertain about what to do with himself, and not sure that there is anything worth doing. The theme of life's meaninglessness is the one that critics such as Edmund Wilson and James E. Miller, Jr. have emphasized.

> In *The Beautiful and Damned,* [writes Miller] Fitzgerald's major theme, as Edmund Wilson indicated, is the meaninglessness of life. The story shows, or was meant to show, the "decay" of his hero, Anthony Patch: "a man of delicate organization in revolt against the inexplicable tragedy of existence." [5]

Miller believes that Fitzgerald fell under the influence of Mencken when he was writing this novel. He refers to Mencken's belief that the "mandates and vagaries of God" are indiscernible, that life is primarily pain, and that "the theme of the great bulk of superior fiction," from Dostoevsky to Dreiser, is "character in decay." "In nearly all the first-rate novels," says Mencken, "the hero is defeated. In perhaps a majority he is completely destroyed." [6]

Miller goes on to point out that *The Beautiful and*

Damned is also concerned with "the revolt of youth," [7] and he maintains that Fitzgerald was unclear in the thematic purpose of the novel because "the theme of the meaninglessness of life tends to neutralize the theme of revolt." [8]

The novel is thematically unclear, but not perhaps in the terms Mr. Miller suggests. The novel is not really about revolt; or if it is, it is the most amorphous kind of rebellion. Anthony is much too passive and weak-willed to be a rebel, and one cannot easily specify what he is revolting against. Is it the capitalistic system? Hardly, since Anthony never condemns the money he hopes to inherit from his grandfather; Dick Caramel writes lucrative popular fiction; and Maury Noble eventually becomes a successful businessman and marries into money. Is it war and the army? Perhaps. Anthony grumbles about the absurdity of military life, and he is court-martialed when he gets into trouble because he comes back to camp late from an affair he is carrying on in town; but up until then he is a model soldier, working his way up to sergeant and winning a nomination to officer's training.

If *The Beautiful and Damned* is not a novel about revolt, it is also more than a novel about "the meaninglessness of life," despite what Edmund Wilson has said. To be sure, the theme is there, and almost all of the characters give it lip-service: Maury says, "And I shall go on shining as a brilliantly meaningless figure in a meaningless world" [23]. Gloria says, " 'There's only one lesson to be learned from life, anyway. . . . That there's no lesson to be learned from life' " [255]. And Anthony remarks, " 'I don't understand why people think that every young man ought to go downtown and work ten hours a day for the best twenty years of his life at dull, unimaginative work, certainly not altruistic work' " [65]. But none of the characters maintains this pose—for this is what it is, a pose. Dick Caramel loudly asserts, " 'I've always believed that moral values existed, and I alway will' " [420]. Maury Noble goes " 'to work so as t forget that there was nothing worth working for' [410], and we are told that " 'he's making *piles* o money. He's sort of changed since the war' " [409] And Gloria eventually contradicts herself, when sh says to Anthony, " 'I've heard you and Maury, an every one else for whose intellect I have the slightes respect, agree that life as it appears is utterly meaning less. But it's always seemed to me that if I wer unconsciously learning something here it might not b meaningless' " [303]. The theme of meaninglessness i appended to the novel. "Fitzgerald no more believe that life is meaningless than he believes in prohibi tion," said one of the early reviewers. "Yet his nove 'The Beautiful and Damned' could be interprete either as a variation on the now popular futilit theme, or a tract to back up the slogan of th Women's Christian Temperance Union." [9]

In *The Beautiful and Damned*, Fitzgerald wa rewriting "May Day," a story he published in July o 1920 in Mencken's *The Smart Set* and republished i *Tales of the Jazz Age*. Like *The Beautiful an Damned*, "May Day" is poorly plotted and badl motivated, Fitzgerald riding the idea of life's meaning lessness, as if that were an answer in itself to life' problems. "May Day" is the story of Gordon Sterrett whose life, like Anthony's, hits a snag, goes empty and lacks the purpose of worthwhile commitment Edith Bradin, who is in love with Gordon, sees that h has dissipated his talent. From her point of view w have a sense of waste, a sense of what could have been When we first see Gordon, he is jobless, in troubl with a mistress, begging money from a disapprovin and unsympathetic old college friend. In the course o the story, he gets drunk at a college alumni dance marries his mistress the same night, and commit suicide the next morning. Sterrett's relationship wit this girl, his reasons for marrying her, and his suicid are vague and unconvincing. They have no function in the story except to serve in melodramatic opposition to Edith's feelings that life with all its exciting adventure goes on: "Love is fragile—she was thinking —but perhaps the pieces are saved, the things that hovered on lips, that might have been said. The new love words, the tendernesses learned, are treasured up for the next lover." [10] The two states of feeling— Edith's romantic and sentimental, and Gordon's pessimistic and despairing—are never reconciled. One is used merely as a device to heighten the other—the theme of deterioration and life's emptiness underscoring Fitzgerald's belief in the promises of youth and life's meaning. The troubles Fitzgerald had with "May Day" are the ones he will have in writing *The Beautiful and Damned*.

Like Gordon Sterrett, Anthony believes in the futility of life, and he supposedly never finds anything in life worthy of his commitment. His leisure is supposed to have an intellectual basis; or, as Fitzgerald puts it, "In justification of his manner of living there was first, of course, The Meaninglessness of Life" [54]. But with Anthony this is a pose, more pretense than real. Anthony has committed himself irrevocably to something—getting his grandfather's fortune. His life is far from meaningless because he has a sense of expectation, of promise, stemming from the pleasure he gets in dreaming about how he and Gloria will eventually spend their fortune. Perhaps it is because he has the "promise" of this money that Anthony finds no need to commit himself seriously to anything else. Certainly Fitzgerald makes it clear that Anthony and Gloria plan to do "important things" once they inherit Adam Patch's fortune: first, settling on "a gorgeous estate . . . then entering diplomacy or politics, to accomplish, for a while, beautiful and important things" [277].

Fitzgerald could not do away with Anthony's sense of commitment just as he could not do away with his own. *The Beautiful and Damned* may treat of post-war disillusionment, but there is another theme beneath this, stamped in every page like a watermark. *The Beautiful and Damned* is a novel about youth—and the waste of it—and this story follows very much the pattern of Fitzgerald's other fiction.

The first phase of the story depicts the excitement of youth. Anthony is young and handsome; Gloria young and beautiful. Anthony is twenty-five, Gloria twenty-two when we first meet them. Gloria, however, looks younger than twenty-two; Anthony mistakes her for eighteen [62 and 64], and when Maury first meets her at tea, he says, " 'She seemed—well somehow the youngest person there.' " Gloria is the very spirit of youth. Fitzgerald says that she brings back memories of lost youth, for as "she would hurry along Fifth Avenue . . . the doors of the Ritz would revolve, the crowd would divide, fifty masculine eyes would start, stare, as she gave back forgotten dreams to husbands of many obese and comic women" [106]. Anthony and Gloria make youth a way of life " 'Everything I do is in accordance with my ideas,' " says Gloria, " 'to use every minute of these years, when I'm young, in having the best time I possibly can' " [304, cf. also 51]. Such excitement lends itself to a sense of the promise of youth.

The second phase of the novel depicts Anthony and Gloria deceived by this sense of anticipation and euphoria, burning themselves up with riotous living. They felt that fast living will bring no consequences, that youth is something to be drawn upon and spent immediately. "She had thought she would never feel so young again," Fitzgerald says of Gloria, that "this was her night, her world" [247]. They live passively, being borne from party to party by a tide of gay and carefree friends until suddenly their lives turn sour and empty, and they find themselves powerless to do anything about their abandonment. Each riotous party, each empty day, each heated argument drains their energy. One night, drunk and annoyed, Anthony physically restrains Gloria from taking a train back to their house, and they get into a violent argument on the railroad platform. Fitzgerald melodramatically refers to this scene as a "horror," and then suggests that youth is a fixed quantity, that Anthony and Gloria are drawing heavily upon it, and that each scene is "taking relentlessly its modicum of youth" [195]. Anthony and Gloria discover—and this is their principal discovery—that youth is perishable and held in trust. The idea of time in tragic flux is voiced at times by the other characters: " 'We're growing old, Anthony,' " says Maury. " 'Three years to thirty, and then I'm what an undergraduate calls a middle-aged man' " [50]. Sometimes it is voiced, in essay-like paragraphs, by Fitzgerald himself:

> It is in the twenties that the actual momentum of life begins to slacken, and it is a simple soul indeed to whom as many things are significant and meaningful at thirty as ten years before. . . . The unmistakable stigma of humanity touches all those impersonal and beautiful things that only youth ever grasps in their impersonal glory. [169–70]

There is a Keatsian sense of time feeding on life in this novel. " 'There's no beauty,' " says Gloria, " 'without poignancy and there's no poignancy without the feeling that it's going, men, names, books, houses—bound for dust—mortal—' " [167, cf. 214 and 417].[11]

The third phase of the novel depicts Anthony and Gloria in decline,[12] fearing the loss of youth and its sense of promise. Anthony begins to look older than his years [cf. 406, 407, 424, 444] and Gloria's beauty begins to fade [cf. 411]. As his friends and acquaintances become successful authors, movie producers, and businessmen, Anthony feels life slipping by him, and their success "rejoiced him only casually and worried him not a little. It meant that the world was going ahead. . . . And he wanted the world to wait motionless . . ." [121]. Anthony realizes that the race is almost won, and he has not yet begun to run. For Gloria, this sense of lost time comes as a shock when she is turned down for a movie role because she looks too old. Gloria returns home one night to find a letter from Joseph Bloeckman, who had arranged a screen test for her.

> My dear Gloria:
>   We had the test run off yesterday afternoon, and Mr. Debris [the name is significant] seemed to think that for the part he had in mind he needed a younger woman. He said that the acting was not bad, and that there was a small character part supposed to be a very haughty rich widow that he thought you might—[403, cf. also 428]

Gloria was twenty-nine when she received this letter, and according to Fitzgerald, "the world was melting away before her eyes" [403]. This is the turning point in the novel for her. It marks the end of her youth, and everything else in her life is anticlimatic. Fitzgerald never leaves us in doubt that life becomes humdrum, that it loses romance once it loses the lustre of youth: "After the sureties of youth there sets in a period of . . . twilight [where] . . . we value safety above romance" [283–84].

The fourth phase of the novel depicts Anthony and Gloria aware of a terrible sense of waste. Gloria feels that she has wasted her youth even before she takes the screen test. As she approaches her twenty-ninth birthday, Fitzgerald says, "the month assumed an ominous and inescapable significance—making her wonder, through these nebulous half-fevered hours *whether after all she had not wasted her faintly tired beauty*, whether there was such a thing as use for any quality bounded by a harsh and inevitable mortality" [391, italics mine]. As Anthony approaches his twenty-ninth birthday, he also is overcome by this same sense of waste, heightened in his case by the success of his friends and old classmates, and "in his moments of insecurity he was haunted by the suggestion that life might be, after all, significant":

> [A] gradual change had taken place through the past several years, accelerated by a succession of anxieties preying on his mind. There was, first of all, the sense of waste, always dormant in his heart. [284]

Over and over, Fitzgerald talks about wasted youth; and the theme of the novel is more than just "the meaninglessness of life."

The Beautiful and Damned is a story about wasted youth—wasted because it was improperly committed. Fitzgerald himself, in describing the reasons for Anthony's abandonment, talks about "a sense of time rushing by, ceaselessly and wastefully" [93]. And with the waste comes the sense of regret. Anthony suffers "nightmares of indecision and regret" [282]. He drinks more heavily in an attempt to keep his sense of youth alive [cf. 417]; and when he realizes that it is gone, the knowledge seems to overwhelm him. Gloria also pathetically and regretfully tries to recapture her lost youth and beauty. "Each night when she prepared for bed she smeared her face with some new unguent which she hoped illogically would give back the glow and freshness to her vanishing beauty" [416]. She reads Galsworthy "whom she liked for his power of recreating, by spring in darkness, that illusion of young romantic love to which women look forever forward and forever backward" [371]. And she thinks often of the past, "imagining how different things might have turned out" [337].

The fifth phase of the novel depicts this sense of what might have been. Anthony and Gloria ache for time past, and their nostilgia stems from the loss of a point of view, a way of looking at reality, as well as from the physical loss of youth. As Fitzgerald says of Anthony, "the gray veil had come down in earnest upon him. As he grew older those things faded—after that there was wine" [417]. At this point, hope and promise are matters of past tense. Fitzgerald's imagination gave absolute consent to this view of youth and life, and it becomes a central theme and a recurrent narrative pattern of his novels.

When Anthony and Gloria reach an advanced state of decline, Adam Patch disinherits them. This is the crudest kind of narrative device. Anthony and Gloria lose their money at the same moment they lose "youth," and Fitzgerald tries to heighten the loss of youth to tragic proportions. In *The Great Gatsby*, Nick Carraway will turn "thirty" the night that Gatsby loses Daisy and the dream, and Fitzgerald will use the same narrative trick again. In *The Great Gatsby*, however, Nick's attitude toward Gatsby is ambivalent—he is both embarrassed and fond of Gatsby; one emotion helps control the other; and we do not have the overstated emotion, the melodrama, of *The Beautiful and Damned*. When Anthony and Gloria break the old man's will and come into a fortune, this is irony in its worst sense. They have lost youth and beauty and have only thirty million dollars to take its place. Fitzgerald would like us to believe they are damned.

Meaning opposed to the meaninglessness of life and youth opposed to the ravages of time—Fitzgerald really has two separate themes in *The Beautiful and Damned*, but he treats them as one, unable to see that they are distinct, and unable to find the means to dramatize them convincingly.

IN A LETTER to Maxwell Perkins from Rome, dated
December 20, 1924, Fitzgerald discussed the creation
of *The Great Gatsby*, which he was then in the
process of revising. After mentioning Tom Buchanan,
Gatsby, Daisy, and Myrtle, Fitzgerald says: "Jordan
Baker of course was a great idea (perhaps you know
it's Edith Cummings)." [1] Edith Cummings was, as I
have already mentioned, a close friend of Ginevra
King, both in Chicago and at Westover where they
were in the class of 1917. Like Jordan Baker, in *The
Great Gatsby*, she was a famous golfer—playing out
of the elegant Onwentsia Club in Chicago—and once
winning the national woman's golf championship.
Fitzgerald met Edith Cummings a number of times—
both in Lake Forest and in New York—when he was
dating Ginevra King.

Fitzgerald met Ginevra when she was invited to St.
Paul by Marie Hersey, and he described their first
meeting—on January 4, 1915 at a dinner dance at the
Town and Country Club—in "Babes in the Woods,"
published in the *Nassau Literary Magazine* in May of
1917 and later included in *This Side of Paradise*. He
later described the unhappy end of this love in "The
Debutante," *Nassau Literary Magazine*, January,
1917. Ginevra encouraged Fitzgerald for a while, along
with many other boys. In June of 1915, they met in
New York and went to *Nobody Home* and the

Midnight Frolic. In March of 1916, Ginevra was expelled from Westover by Miss Hillard, the headmistress. Fourteen years later, in September of 1930, Fitzgerald was still interested enough in Ginevra to write a short story about her expulsion, entitled "A Woman with a Past," for the *Saturday Evening Post*. This later became one of the Josephine stories and was included in *Taps at Reveille*.

In the story, Josephine is put on probation by a Miss Kwain who maintained that Josephine was flirting with boys calling to her from under her dormitory window. Soon after, while walking with Ernest Waterbury near the campus chapel, Josephine "slipped" into his "unwilling arms, where she lay helpless, convulsed with irresistible laughter. It was in this position that Miss Brereton and the visiting trustee had found them." [2] Miss Brereton expelled Josephine and then retracted, just as Miss Hillard had expelled Ginevra and then retracted. Neither Ginevra nor Josephine, however, would return to the school.

In August of 1916, Fitzgerald visited Ginevra in Lake Forest. Peg Carry, Edith Cummings, Courtney Letts—the old Westover crowd—were all there, and, according to Fitzgerald's Ledger, there was a "petting party" and many gay evenings. The Kings made it clear that they disapproved of Fitzgerald. In his Ledger, Fitzgerald wrote that someone at this time told him, "Poor boys shouldn't think of marrying rich girls." [3] If Mr. King would not put it this crudely, these were his sentiments. [4]

The next time that Fitzgerald saw Ginevra King was with Peg Carry at the Yale game in November of 1916. Ginevra met Fitzgerald once again in January of 1917, at which time she broke with him for good.

The conclusion of "A Woman with a Past" is thus pure daydream. When Josephine leaves school, she goes to Hot Springs where she meets a young man who "had flunked out of Princeton in February" [195]. (Fitzgerald had not exactly "flunked out" of

Princeton, but the reference is obvious.) Josephine learns at Hot Springs something that Nick Carraway learns in *The Great Gatsby*—that playing with other's affections has moral consequences: "One mustn't run through people . . . for the sake of a romantic half-hour" [199]. The moment she realizes this she sees Mr. Gordon Tinsley, from Yale, "the current catch of Chicago, reputedly the richest young man in the Middle West. He had never paid any attention to young Josephine until tonight. Ten minutes ago he had asked her to go driving with him" [199]. She rejects him because "the Princeton man was still at her ear, still imploring her to walk out with him into the night" [199–200].

It did not happen this way in life. In June of 1917, Fitzgerald suspected that Ginevra was engaged; in September of 1917, he wrote in his Ledger, "Oh Ginevra"; by June of 1918, while he was stationed at Camp Sheridan near Montgomery, Alabama, he found out that Ginevra King was to be married in September. She was marrying William Mitchell who, like Gordon Tinsley in the story, was "the current catch of Chicago." Mitchell was from an extremely wealthy family, long associated with Chicago banking —especially with the Continental Illinois Bank. After he married Ginevra, Mitchell became a director in the family firm of Mitchell, Hutchins & Co., and served on the boards of Balaban and Katz, Inland Glass, and Elgin Clock.

Ginevra King's father, like Josephine's father, went to Yale (class of 1894), and Charles King and William Mitchell both owned a string of polo ponies, Mr. King bringing his East to Long Island where he often rode with Louis E. Stoddard who was on the American team that played England in the twenties. The principal characters in *The Great Gatsby* thus begin to emerge: a great deal of Ginevra King went into Fitzgerald's conception of Daisy Fay; Tom Buchanan —who came from a wealthy Chicago family, went to

Yale, owned a string of polo ponies on Long Island—is the fusion of Mr. King and William Mitchell; Jordan Baker is Edith Cummings, a friend of Ginevra, just as Jordan is a friend of Daisy.

Fitzgerald came away from Ginevra with a sense of social inadequacy, a deep hurt, and longing for the girl beyond attainment. He expressed these sentiments first, not in *The Great Gatsby*, but in "Winter Dreams," published in December of 1922 in *Metropolitan Magazine*. In this story, the two lovers are separated by money—Dexter Green is the son of a grocer, just as Fitzgerald's maternal grandfather was in the grocery business—and Judy Jones's father is as wealthy as his Pierce-Arrow automobile indicates. When he is twenty-three, Dexter falls in love with Judy, who encourages and then drops him. At twenty-five Dexter is engaged to another girl, but he breaks his engagement when Judy once again shows interest in him. When Judy has proved to herself her complete power over Dexter, she dismisses him once and for all from her life. At thirty-two, Dexter is a Jay Gatsby, preserving his "old" image of Judy, his "winter" dreams: Dexter learns at this time that Judy, who has since married, is having marital troubles and that she has "faded" and is considered "too old" for her husband. The news shocks him because suddenly he realizes that his youth is gone—and with it an ideal conception of perfect beauty that had kept the world resplendent and alive:

> He had thought that having nothing else to lose he was invulnerable at last—but he knew that he had just lost something more, as surely as if he had married Judy Jones and seen her fade away before his eyes.
> The dream was gone. Something had been taken from him. . . . For he had gone away and he could never go back any more. . . . Even the grief he could have borne was left behind in the country of illusion, of youth . . . where his winter dreams had flourished.
> "Long ago," he said, "long ago, there was something

in me, but now that thing is gone. . . . I cannot cry. I cannot care. That thing will come back no more." [5]

As in "Winter Dreams," Fitzgerald gets his feelings of lost youth and beauty into *The Great Gatsby*. He also gets into the novel his sense of social inadequacy and his emotion of hurt when the dream is betrayed by lack of money. "'The whole idea of Gatsby,'" Fitzgerald said, "'is the unfairness of a poor young man not being able to marry a girl with money. This theme comes up again and again because I lived it.'" [6]

Fitzgerald had almost lost Zelda also because of his lack of money; but he finally won her. It was the wound over Ginevra that never healed (Fitzgerald described it "as the skin wound on a haemophile"). Fitzgerald kept all of Ginevra's letters to the end of his life. He even had them typed up and bound in a volume that runs 227 pages.

The "dreams" in "Winter Dreams" are an eternal yearning for the promise of summer and the fulfillment of romance. When Fitzgerald lost Ginevra, he came to believe that such yearning was an end in itself; he believed in the need to preserve a romantic state of mind where the imagination and the will are arrested—in a state of suspension—by an idealized concept of beauty and love. The loss creates an eternal striving, and hope keeps the world beautifully alive.

When Gatsby kisses Daisy his mind "would never romp again," his conception of beauty was fixed, and his will yearned eternally for that beauty. "It is sadder to find the past again," Fitzgerald once wrote, "and find it inadequate to the present than it is to have it elude you and remain forever a harmonious conception of memory." [7]

As long as one cares, the loss can keep the world alive with expectation. Nick Carraway expresses Gatsby's loss of expectation when he surmises that perhaps Gatsby "no longer cared" and if so, then his sky must have suddenly become "unfamiliar," the leaves "frightening," and a rose "grotesque." As Daisy was the source of Gatsby's ideal beauty, Ginevra King was the source of Fitzgerald's. In October of 1937, when he was writing for Hollywood, Fitzgerald went up to Santa Barbara to see Ginevra who was there on a visit. He was overcome with fear because "She was the first girl I ever loved and I have faithfully avoided seeing her up to this moment to keep that illusion perfect." [8]

Fitzgerald saw the need for a "perfect illusion" as part of the creative impulse. In "The Pierian Spring and the Last Straw," an early (1917) short story, the author gets his girl and then no longer feels the need to write. Not only did Ginevra King go into *The Great Gatsby*; she was in many ways part of Fitzgerald's motive for writing the novel in the first place. Is it any wonder that at one point in *The Great Gatsby* Daisy Fay is described as "the king's daughter"?

In the same passage in which Fitzgerald tells us that Jordan Baker is modelled on Edith Cummings, he also tells us that "after careful searching of the files (of a man's mind here) for the Fuller Magee [sic] case and after having Zelda draw pictures until her fingers ache I know Gatsby better than I know my own child." [9]

There has been a great deal of confusion about the real life model for Gatsby. George Jean Nathan tells us that Fitzgerald asked to be introduced to a bootlegger. Nathan introduced him to two—one named Nicky Bates—but they did not match Fitzgerald's imaginative conception of a bootlegger. [10] Fitzgerald eventually seems to have met a bootlegger more to his liking. He told Edmund Wilson about this man, and Wilson supposedly described him in his play *The Crime in the Whistler Room*:

> He's a gentleman bootlegger: his name is Max Fleischman. He lives like a millionaire. Gosh, I haven't seen so much to drink since Prohibition. . . . Well, Fleischman was making a damn ass of himself bragging about

how much his tapestries were worth and how much his bath-room was worth and how he never wore a shirt twice—and he had a revolver studded with diamonds. . . . And he finally got on my nerves—I was a little bit stewed—and I told him I wasn't impressed by his ermine-lined revolver: I told him he was nothing but a bootlegger, no matter how much money he made. . . . I told him I never would have come into his damn house if it hadn't been to be polite and that it was torture to stay in a place where everything was in such terrible taste.[11]

This description, however, does not explain Fitzgerald's interest in the Fuller-McGee case (Fitzgerald had misspelled McGee's name), an interest which is of further importance because Fitzgerald knew Fuller who lived in Great Neck, Long Island when the Fitzgeralds lived there in 1922 and 1923.

The Fuller-McGee case began quietly enough. Tucked away in the November 14 (Tuesday) 1922 issue of the *New York Times* between an item about the annual report of Crucible Steel Company of America and foreign securities was a nine-line item about Edward M. Fuller and William Frank McGee:

The examination of witnesses at the trial of Edward M. Fuller of the bankrupt firm of E. M. Fuller and Co. will begin today in General Sessions. William F. McGee, a co-defendant with Fuller, on an indictment charging bucketing of orders, will have a separate trial. The jury in Fuller's case was completed yesterday.[12]

The case came about when Franklin B. Link of Westmoreland, Tennessee, charged Fuller and McGee of bucketing his order for $1,500 worth of Middle States Oil stock. At this point, Fuller and McGee declared bankruptcy. After an examination of the firm's books, the liabilities of Fuller and McGee were first set at five million dollars and later at slightly less than two million ($1,888,812).

The Fuller-McGee scheme seems to have worked this way: A. J. Harold Braid, of the brokerage firm of Braid and Vogel on the New York Exchange, allowed his name to be used in making stock transactions for which he received two dollars per share of business. An Albert Biehman, a clerk for Fuller and McGee, would take the prices of stock from the ticker tape, quote the prices to the customers, take the customers' orders, but never make the transactions to a broker, "bucketing" the money for Fuller and McGee.

This practice was not new. Since 1917 scores of brokerage firms had gone bankrupt in New York with liabilities of more than 150 million dollars. These companies would sell stock on worthless businesses—especially mineral mines. As long as such "mines" existed and people were willing to buy their stock, this was not illegal. These same brokerage firms, however, often accepted money on legitimate stock and then "bucketed"—that is, pocketed—the money and never completed the customer's order. This was extremely profitable—and extremely illegal.

The four trials of Fuller and McGee were a series of farces. The first trial resulted in a hung jury. The second was declared a mistrial because J. Harold Braid, the state's principal witness, disappeared. The third trial—in which four witnesses and important documents disappeared—also resulted in a hung verdict, the grand jury later investigating attempts to bribe one of the jurors. The fourth trial, which resulted in the conviction of Fuller and McGee, also brought Arnold Rothstein on the stage when it was learned that Rothstein had "borrowed" $187,000 from Edward Fuller. Later investigation showed that Rothstein was the man behind Fuller and McGee from the very beginning.

When the warrants were first issued, and Fuller and McGee were charged with "bucketing," they could not be found. Arthur Garfield Hays, in his *City Lawyer*, describes how he was summoned to assist Fuller and McGee:

> After the bankruptcy of E. M. Fuller and Company, the assets, Fuller, and McGee all vanished. A few weeks

later a telephone call summoned me to a brownstone house of the upper West Side. I asked who lived there. "Arnold Rothstein." . . . Fuller and McGee were comfortably living in Rothstein's home, waiting for the storm to subside. They were expecting Bill Fallon [another attorney] that afternoon.[13]

Arnold Rothstein, of course, is the model for Meyer Wolfsheim in *The Great Gatsby*. Rothstein had moved from small time gambler to become king of the New York bookmakers, the proprietor of a big gambling hotel, and the owner of a profitable racing stable. He was also the man behind New York bootlegging and behind the bucket shops. He was, furthermore, as Nick Carraway learns about Meyer Wolfsheim, the man who fixed the World Series in 1919. As Nick Carraway had met Meyer Wolfsheim, Fitzgerald had met Rothstein—and the meeting left an indeliable impression on his imagination. Fitzgerald recalled in July of 1937:

> In *Gatsby* I selected the stuff to fit a given mood or "hauntedness" or whatever you might call it, rejecting in advance in *Gatsby*, for instance, all of the ordinary material for Long Island, big crooks, adultery theme and always starting from the *small* focal point that impressed me—my own meeting with Arnold Rothstein for instance.[14]

Fitzgerald knew both Rothstein and Fuller, and there is in *The Great Gatsby* the same relationship between Meyer Wolfsheim and his lieutenant, Jay Gatsby, as there was in real life between Rothstein and his lieutenant, Edward Fuller. When Fitzgerald said that Gatsby "started as one man I knew and then changed into myself," [15] that man was Edward Fuller, Fitzgerald's Great Neck neighbor (just as Nick is Gatsby's West Egg neighbor).

Fitzgerald could depict Gatsby (Fuller) as a bootlegger, since Rothstein (Wolfsheim) controlled New York bootlegging. But Gatsby is more than a bootlegger—and Fitzgerald makes it clear that Gatsby, like Edward Fuller, was in the bond business, a point that most of the critics have never noticed. When Gatsby asks Nick to arrange the meeting with Daisy, he suggests that he can help Nick who is also selling bonds:

"I carry on a little business on the side, a sort of side line, you understand. And I thought that if you don't make very much—You're selling bonds, aren't you, old sport?"
"Trying to."
"Well, this would interest you. It wouldn't take up much of your time and you might pick up a nice bit of money. It happens to be a rather confidential sort of thing." [16]

When Tom confronts Gatsby at the Plaza hotel, he insinuates that Gatsby's business is more than just bootlegging. "That drug-store business was just small change,' continued Tom slowly, 'but you've got something on now that Walter's afraid to tell me about' " [135]. And when Nick answers the phone, after Gatsby's death, the unsuspecting caller tells him:

"Young Parke's in trouble," he said rapidly. "They picked him up when he handed the bonds over the counter. They got a circular from New York giving 'em the numbers just five minutes before. What d'you know about that, hey? You never can tell in these hick towns —" [one may recall at this point Gatsby's phone conversations about small towns]. [167]

Why Fitzgerald chose to model Gatsby on a crooked stock broker is an interesting question. One answer is that perhaps this was Fitzgerald's private joke—a subtle way of getting back at Charles King and William Mitchell, both of whom were in the bond business. By modelling Gatsby on Edward Fuller, and then by allowing Gatsby to embody many of his own feelings, Fitzgerald was ironically depicting the gap between himself and the Kings-Mitchells. In this way, Jay Gatsby of West Egg becomes comically related to Tom Buchanan of East Egg; one is the ersatz parallel of the other.

In an apprentice story, "The Pierian Springs and the Last Straw" (*Nassau Literary Magazine*, October, 1917), George Rombert has many of the qualities of *both* Jay Gatsby and Tom Buchanan. Like Gatsby, he loses the love of his life when he is betrayed by his "emotional imagination"; and when he loses his girl, time stops: " 'When I crossed the threshold,' " he says, " 'it was sixteen minutes after ten. At that minute I stopped living.' " [17] Like Buchanan, George Rombert is an overbearing bully. In *The Great Gatsby* Daisy accuses Tom of bruising her finger, and in this early story George Rombert breaks Myra's finger. The narrator of the story, another parallel to *The Great Gatsby*, has the same reservations about George Rombert that Nick Carraway has about Tom Buchanan, and he is not afraid to pass moral judgment: "My Uncle's [George Rombert's] personality had dropped off him like a cloak. He was not the romantic figure of the grill, but a less sure, less attractive and somewhat contemptible individual." [172] Myra's husband, we are told, is a broker—a "crooked broker," according to George Rombert, a " 'damn thief that robbed me of everything in this hellish world' " [172–73]. In "The Pierian Springs and the Last Straw" we have the germ of Jay Gatsby and Tom Buchanan—and the theme of the "crooked broker." Fitzgerald later gave Tom and Gatsby separate qualities—modelling Gatsby on Edward Fuller, and Tom on William Mitchell-Charles King. His models, however, were all brokers; and in *The Great Gatsby* there is an amusing, although slightly hidden, relationship between Gatsby and Tom Buchanan—both were, at least in conception, "crooked brokers." The broker will steal the object of love in Fitzgerald's late as well as early fiction. Tommy Barban, who takes Nicole Warren away from Dick Diver in *Tender Is the Night*, is, among other things, a broker.

Fitzgerald also saw that Edward Fuller's social

position was a kind of grotesque embodiment of his own. He was rejected by Ginevra for being socially inferior. Fitzgerald extended the difference between himself and Ginevra by making Gatsby into the essence of the social impostor. At one point in *The Great Gatsby*, when Daisy seems about ready to leave Tom for Gatsby, they hear—ironically enough—the chords of Mendelssohn's Wedding March from the ballroom of the Plaza hotel. Daisy suddenly remembers a man named Biloxi, who fainted at their wedding, and they discover that each thought that the other knew him. Biloxi, in fact, told Daisy that he was president of Tom's class at Yale. Biloxi, the impostor, embodies the very spirit of Gatsby in the world of Tom Buchanan. Tom, in fact, asks Gatsby if he went to Oxford "about the time Biloxi went to New Haven" [129]. Biloxi, like Gatsby, is an exaggerated expression of Fitzgerald's own feelings with the high rich of Lake Forest and elsewhere.

Fitzgerald was doing something in *The Great Gatsby* that he had not done before. He was pushing his sense of experience away from the middle ground of verisimilitude toward extremes—toward two kinds of distortions. The dreamer distorted becomes Gatsby —a man whose hopelessly vulgar taste allows an eternal yearning for a meretricious beauty. The rich man distorted becomes Tom Buchanan—a man whose ruthlessness preserves his wordly comfort, and whose shoddy ideas keep intact his sense of superiority. Both Gatsby and Tom Buchanan are men without conscience. Gatsby is just as intent on taking Daisy from Tom as Tom is on keeping Daisy from Gatsby. Both caricature Fitzgerald's own experience—his own sense of combat: the dreamer in conflict with a rigid reality; the promises of youth in conflict with the ravages of time; and the man of suspect means in conflict with the established rich.

These were the themes that Fitzgerald rehearsed in his short stories. In fact, he would use the short stories to work out—sometimes through fantasy, other times through a straight-forward handling of the situation—what in the novels he would treat through irony and with symbolic overtone.

"The Jelly Bean," for example, published in the October 1920 issue of *Metropolitan Magazine*, reveals a Georgian roustabout falling in love with a beautiful but wild young flapper who runs away and marries another man after an evening of dancing and hard drinking. The story is not very profound, but the major themes are here: the poignant distance between the rich and the poor, the glamor that arouses youthful commitment, and the death of the dream—in this case before it is born.

" 'O Russet Witch,' " published in the February 1922 issue of *Metropolitan Magazine*, is a fantasy story about a young clerk who falls in love with Caroline—the spirit of youth, ideal beauty, and adventure—loses her, accepts a more prosaic wife, and settles down to a workaday routine until he suddenly realizes that he is thirty and entering that "sordid and always gray decade of worry and failing enthusiasm and failing dreams, years when the moonlight had grown duller in the areaway and the youth had faded out of Olive's face." [18]

"The Curious Case of Benjamin Button," published in the May 1922 issue of *Collier's*, was another fantasy story concerned with the theme of time and the promises of youth. Benjamin is supposedly seventy years old when he is born, and he lives his life in reverse. The brightest moment in his life comes fifty years after his birth, when he scores seven touchdowns and fourteen field goals for Harvard in the Yale game. After this, Benjamin begins to weaken, enters childhood, and finally dies a helpless infant in a crib.

"The Diamond as Big as the Ritz," published in the June 1922 issue of *Smart Set*, is still another fantasy treatment of *The Great Gatsby* themes and situation. Based on Fitzgerald's own trip to the Montana ranch of Charles (Sap) Donahoe, a friend from Newman, the story embellishes Fitzgerald's own experience. On a diamond mountain, John T. Unger (jaunty hunger) falls in love with Kismine Washington, who tells him that no guest ever left the mountain alive. Like the slaves kept in an underground prison (the hell of middle-class life), the guests must be "sacrificed"—as Gatsby and Dick Diver will be sacrificed—so the Washington (the reference is obviously to George Washington and the idea of success in America) family can stay comfortably intact. When the mountain is blown up, John loses the dream—the hope of arresting an idealized moment of time, the resplendent moment that comes with the eternal promise of youth. Kismine says, " 'I always thought of [the stars] as great big diamonds that belonged to someone. Now they frighten me. They make me feel that it was all a dream, all my youth.' " John responds, " 'It *was* a dream. . . . Everybody's youth is a dream.' " [19]

In "Winter Dreams," published in the December 1922 issue of *Metropolitan Magazine*, Fitzgerald, as we have already seen, described, through Dexter Green and Judy Jones, the same sense of loss that he felt over Ginevra King, that Gatsby felt over Daisy. The emphasis is again upon youth—Dexter Green has the ineffable longings of a Fitzgerald hero for the past, for the moments of youth with their special and privileged point of view, for the lost moment that can never be relived.

Fitzgerald brings this same obsession with lost youth to "The Sensible Thing," a story he published in the July 1924 issue of *Liberty*. George O'Kelly graduated from the Massachusetts Institute of Technology, accepted an engineering job in Tennessee, and fell in love with the young and beautiful Jonquil Cary. When she will not marry him, he quits his job and goes to New York, hoping to make money in the insurance business, just as Fitzgerald went to New York, hoping to make money in advertising, when

Zelda would not marry him. He fails in New York, "his dream slipping fast behind";[20] goes back to Tennessee where Jonquil breaks with him; and then leaves for Peru where he makes a fortune but loses his youth. Even though Jonquil will probably marry him, George feels that he has lost the best part of his life. Throughout the story, fans whir "like a clock ticking" [224], dusk descends upon "the flowers of his young world" [229], and he feels "a warmth [has] gone forever" [235].

"Absolution," of course, is the short story most directly related to *The Great Gatsby* because it was originally intended to be a part of the novel before Fitzgerald extracted and published it in the June 1924 issue of Mencken's *American Mercury*. Rudolph Miller, who is Jay Gatsby as a child, lives by Father Schwartz's dictum of not getting too close to reality because " 'you'll only feel the heat and sweat of life.' "[21] When Rudolph lied in the confessional, he was only "brightening up the dinginess of his admissions" [131]. Rudolph walks in the light of his own imagination; like Dexter Green he has the dreams of youth, and like Jay Gatsby he has created out of these dreams an idealized image of himself. Yet Rudolph, Dexter, and Gatsby are all subject to time. " 'Do you hear the hammer and the clock and the bees?' " asks Father Schwartz. " 'Well, that's no good' " [128]. Gatsby also never heard the clock, and, as "Absolution" suggests, he was the victim of his own imagination—and of lost youth.

The Great Gatsby begins in the spring of 1922. Fitzgerald is very careful to specify the ages of his characters. Gatsby is "a year or two over thirty" [48]. Tom Buchanan is just thirty [7]. Daisy is twenty-three, and Jordan Baker is twenty-one [cf. 75]. And Nick Carraway is twenty-nine.

When Gatsby was seventeen, he met Dan Cody, a kind of pioneer, grown fabulously rich from mining interests, and for five years he was Cody's "steward,

mate, skipper, secretary, and even jailor" [101]. Dan
Cody is another grotesque embodiment—this time of
James J. Hill (1838–1916)—who was the wealthiest
man in St. Paul and whose mansion, across from the
cathedral which sits on a hill overlooking the whole
city, was on the opposite end of Summit Avenue from
the house in which Fitzgerald lived most of his
adolescent life, just as Gatsby's house is across the bay
from the Buchanan's.

Hill was born in Ontario and settled in St. Paul
when he arrived several days too late to join a brigade
of trappers and traders adventuring in 1856 across the
West. He made his first money supplying wood and
coal to the railroad, and then in 1878 bought out the
St. Paul and Pacific railroad which he expanded in
1890 into the Great Northern Railway Company.
Like Dan Cody, Hill made a fortune from mining and
mineral interests when he bought the Mesabi ore
range (25,000 acres) in 1899 for slightly over four
million dollars. From 1906 to 1916, the profits from
this venture alone were almost twelve million. At the
end of the novel, Gatsby's father tells Nick that if
Gatsby had "lived, he'd of been a great man. A man
like James J. Hill. He'd of helped build up the
country" [169].

When Gatsby was a twenty-seven-year-old first lieutenant stationed at Camp Taylor, he met and fell in
love with the beautiful Daisy Fay. She returned his
love, wrote to Gatsby while he was overseas, and then
—realizing that Gatsby was penniless—married Tom
Buchanan, who is so wealthy that he could give her a
$350,000 pearl necklace for a wedding present. Gatsby
has a Platonic conception of self—based in part on
being as rich as Dan Cody, and in the main on
marrying Daisy Fay—so to abandon Daisy would be
to lose his sense of self. Nick says, "He talked a lot
about the past, and I gathered that he wanted to
recover something, some idea of himself perhaps, that
had gone into loving Daisy. His life had been con-

fused and disordered since then, but if he could once return to a certain starting place and go over it all slowly, he could find out what that thing was" [111–12]. Gatsby wants to keep his image intact—and without blemish. It does not even satisfy him to think that Daisy remained faithful to his image of her, and that she had never stopped loving him during her five years of marriage. He wants to turn back the clock and to start over at thirty-two where he left off at twenty-seven:

> He wanted nothing less of Daisy than that she should go to Tom and say: "I never loved you." After she had obliterated four years with that sentence they could decide upon the more practical measures to be taken. One of them was that, after she was free, they were to go back to Louisville and be married from her house— just as if it were five years ago. [111]

Nick knows that Daisy can never come up to Gatsby's imaginative expectations. "Daisy tumbled short of his dreams," says Nick, "not through her own fault, but because of the colossal vitality of his illusion. It had gone beyond her, beyond everything" [97]. Nick also knows that one cannot obliterate time, that in those five years Daisy and Tom have known love, and that at thirty-two the illusions of twenty-seven have lost their promise:

> "I wouldn't ask too much of her," [Nick] ventured. "You can't repeat the past."
> "Can't repeat the past?" [Gatsby] cried incredulously. "Why of course you can!" [111]

Gatsby cannot repeat the past, just as Anthony Patch could not buy back his lost youth. As Nick says at the end of the novel, Gatsby "had come a long way . . . and his dream must have seemed so close that he could hardly fail to grasp it. He did not know that it was already behind him" [182].

The crisis in *The Great Gatsby* comes in "the

parlor of a suite in the Plaza Hotel" [126], one horribly hot late afternoon in August of 1922. Tom, Daisy, Gatsby, Nick, and Jordan Baker have motored in from East Egg, and Gatsby and Daisy tell Tom that they are in love. Gatsby tries to get Daisy to admit that she never loved Tom, but she cannot do this: " 'Oh, you want too much!' she cried to Gatsby. 'I love you now—isn't that enough? I can't help what's past.' She began to sob helplessly. 'I did love him once—but I loved you too' " [133]. The word "too" makes Gatsby shudder, and his dream begins to fall apart. When Tom tells Daisy that Gatsby's "drugstores" are really a front for his bootlegging operations, and when he hints at Gatsby's other schemes, the dream is dead. Daisy will never give up the security of established Buchanan money for the tenuous and illegal fortune Gatsby has amassed as Meyer Wolfsheim's lieutenant. Gatsby tries to argue with Daisy, "But with every word she was drawing further and further into herself, so he gave that up, and only the dead dream fought on as the afternoon slipped away" [135].

Daisy asks Tom to take her home, and Tom, confident that Daisy is forever his, tells her to go back to East Egg with Gatsby. As Nick is about to leave, Tom asks him if he wants any of the whiskey. Nick answers no, and without transition adds, " 'I just remembered that today's my birthday. I was thirty' " [136].

Gatsby loses more than Daisy and the dream that hot August afternoon; he also loses the spirit of youth, the eternal hope, the sense of expectancy and promise that Fitzgerald predicated of the age between seventeen and thirty. And Nick Carraway also feels an excitement go out of his life. Although Nick tells us that Gatsby is the object of his "scorn" [2], he is taken by Gatsby's "heightened sensitivity to the promises of life" [2]. And when the promise of life dies for Gatsby, it does for Nick too:

Thirty—the promise of a decade of loneliness, [he says] a thinning list of single men to know, a thinning briefcase of enthusiasm, thinning hair. But there was Jordan beside me, who, unlike Daisy, was too wise ever to carry well-forgotten dreams from age to age. As we passed over the dark bridge her wan face fell lazily against my coat's shoulder and the formidable stroke of thirty died away with the reassuring pressure of her hand. [136]

In *This Side of Paradise*, Amory asks, "but isn't it lack of willpower to let my imagination shiny on the wrong side?" In *The Beautiful and Damned* Fitzgerald dramatized man's fight against the ravages of time. In *The Great Gatsby* the themes merge. Fitzgerald depicts the dreamer—vulgar and tasteless—trying to turn back the clock. His hopeless task, his fidelity of purpose, even the shoddiness of the dream itself—all combine to make Gatsby's attempt poignant and touching. Gatsby is a Sisyphus without self-knowledge or cosmic understanding.

The dimension that Fitzgerald adds to *The Great Gatsby* is irony. Nick Carraway is repulsed by and attracted to Gatsby. He is repulsed by the man's vulgar taste and gaudy display; he is attracted by the sincerity of Gatsby and his fidelity of commitment. He is repulsed by the Buchanans' *droit de seigneur* and their moral carelessness; he is attracted by their mobility and their heightened life. When Nick encouraged Jordan Baker—who is much like the Buchanans—he is giving emotional consent to their world. Fitzgerald was caricaturing his own experience —especially at Lake Forest, where he felt like a poor boy in a rich man's world. Through Nick Carraway, Fitzgerald is able to bring to the surface two ambivalent facets of his own character—his sense of life's promise and his fear of wasting time; his distrust of the very rich and his envy of their larger life. Gatsby embodies that element in Fitzgerald which gave enthusiastic and unexamined consent to the wonder of

life. Nick embodies that other element in Fitzgerald
which became excited by life's possibility but was
prone to brood over the past and to be irredeemably
hurt by disappointment. Nick embodies Fitzgerald's
character from both inside and out, as both the agent
of his experience and the object of analysis, as both
seeing and seen. "I was within and without," Nick
says at the New York apartment on 158th Street,
"simultaneously enchanted and repelled by the inexhaustible variety of life" [36]. We see through Nick
what is shoddy and glamorous in both Gatsby and the
Buchanans, and this antithetical juxtaposition is the
source of the novel's irony. Nick as ironic narrator is
constantly tugged at—attracted and repelled by the
same experience. The only character in the novel who
puts experience to the scrutiny of an active conscience, Nick can say at one and the same time that
"there was something gorgeous about" Gatsby and
that Gatsby "represented everything for which I have
an unaffected scorn" [2].

Nick might have eventually married Jordan if
Gatsby had not been murdered by George Wilson. He
finds out that Tom sent Wilson to Gatsby's house
knowing that Wilson would murder him. Nick saw
Daisy and Tom "conspiring" after Daisy ran over
Myrtle Wilson in Gatsby's car, and he suspects that
Tom knew Daisy and not Gatsby was doing the
driving. The Buchanans use Gatsby; ruthlessly sacrificed him, and one of the final ironies of the novel is
that Gatsby had to die so that Daisy and Tom could
live on." "They were careless people, Tom and
Daisy," says Nick, "they smashed up things and
creatures and then retreated back into their money or
their vast carelessness, or whatever it was that kept
them together, and let other people clean up the mess
they had made" [180–81]. And because Nick guesses
the truth about Tom and Daisy, he breaks off with
Jordan, who is very much—in her supercilious, overbearing, careless way—a Buchanan. When she is

FITZGERALD dedicated *Tender Is the Night* to Gerald
and Sara Murphy, and it is commonly known that
Fitzgerald modelled Dick and Nicole Diver, in part,
on the Murphys. Murphy, whose father was president
of Mark Cross (the New York leather goods store),
went to Yale, was in the top fraternity (DKE), a
member of Skull and Bones, and an important man in
the class of 1911.

In 1922 the Murphys went to Paris where they
became friends of writers, artists, and diplomats.
When Stravinsky's ballet "Les Noces" premièred in
1923, they gave a party on a barge tied up to a dock in
the Seine, and included in the forty guests were
Picasso, Darius Milhaud, Jean Cocteau, Ernest Anser-
met, Diaghilev, Tristram Tzara, and Scofield Thayer
(editor of the *Dial*).[1]

In the summer of 1923, Cole Porter invited the
Murphys down to his rented château at Cap
d'Antibes. After May first, the tourists left Antibes
because it was too hot. The Murphys, however, fell in
love with it. Gerald dug out a corner of the beach,
convinced the owner of a small hotel to stay open
. . . . keleton staff, and stayed on for the summer.

. . . . ld met the Murphys in Paris the next year,
. . . . was inevitable that Murphy would impress
. . . . d whose imagination could warm to his social
. . . . asy manner, and heightened way of life.

"When I like men," Fitzgerald once wrote, "I want to be like them—I want to lose the outer qualities that give me my individuality and be like them." [2] Fitzgerald acted upon such a desire when he made Dick Diver a composite of Gerald Murphy and himself.

As *Tender Is the Night* opens, Dick Diver is really Gerald Murphy at Cap d'Antibes, raking red seaweed from the beach, keeping his guests amused, and being the emotional nucleus of the group, the object of Rosemary Hoyt's admiring eyes. Fitzgerald partly modelled Gausse's hotel on the Hôtel du Cap d'Antibes. The Villa Diana, where the Divers have their garden party, is a composite of a house owned by Samuel Barlow (an American composer) and the exotic garden of the Villa American, the house the Murphys built in a garden surrounded by orange, lemon, and cedar trees. Nicole at the beginning of the novel, her brown back "set off by a string of creamy pearls," is Sara Murphy who often wore pearls on the beach because she believed the sun was good for them.

A great many of Fitzgerald's experiences went into *Tender Is the Night*. In the winter of 1924, he fought, like Dick Diver, with a group of taxi drivers, punched a policeman in the fracas, and was severely beaten. Late one night on the Riviera, Fitzgerald, like Abe North, threatened to saw a waiter in half. Also, like Abe North, Fitzgerald had his wallet stolen in a Paris night club, accused the wrong Negro, and created an unpleasant scene.[3]

Fitzgerald also brought to the Riviera a number of people who had impressed him in America. Abe North, who prefigures Dick's decline, is based on Ring Lardner. Fitzgerald wrote Maxwell Perkins in January of 1933 that "I am [Ernest Hemingway's] alcoholic just like Ring is mine," [4] and Lardner symbolized for Fitzgerald the man of genius who had dissipated his energy and wasted his talent. When Dick learns one day during his own decline that Abe has been killed—

beaten to death in a speakeasy—"Dick's lungs burst for a moment with regret for Abe's death, and his own youth of ten years ago." [5]

Rosemary Hoyt was modelled on Lois Moran, the movie star, whom Fitzgerald met in 1927 when he was working for United Artists on a story for Constance Talmadge. George Jean Nathan described Lois in much the way Fitzgerald depicted her in *Tender Is the Night:* "She was a lovely kid of such tender years that it was rumored she still wore the kind of flannel nightie that was bound around her ankles with ribbons, and Scott never visited her save when her mother was present." [6]

The *Tender Is the Night* that Fitzgerald published in 1934 is a much different novel from the one he began writing in Juan-les-Pins in 1925. The novel was originally about matricide, based on a 1925 San Francisco murder in which a sixteen-year-old girl, Dorothy Ellingson, killed her mother who objected to her daughter's wild living. [7] Fitzgerald worked on this version from 1925 to 1929. He planned to take liberties with the Ellingson case, setting the novel on the Riviera where Francis Melarky, a young motion picture technician, was to murder his mother, Charlotte Melarky. This version went through four drafts and was variously entitled *Our Type, The Boy who Killed his Mother, The Melarky Case,* and *The World's Fair.*

Sara Murphy may have had Fitzgerald's title in mind when she said of that summer in Antibes: "It was like a great fair, and everybody was so young." [8] *The World's Fair* version, which has since been published, [9] reveals that Francis Melarky is modelled on Fitzgerald himself, and the Pipers (who later become the Divers) are modelled on the Murphys. Francis, in fact, is in love with Dinah Piper, who encourages him. As Arthur Mizener pointed out, the Pipers are depicted ambiguously—favorably from Francis' point of view, unfavorably from Abe Grant's (who becomes Abe North). As in *The Great Gatsby*, the narrator analyzes a magnetic character, and we again have the bifurcated point of view with two resulting emotions—admiration and cynicism—only here the emotions are those of two men rather than one.

In the finished version of *Tender Is the Night*, Fitzgerald fused Francis Melarky (Fitzgerald himself) with Seth Piper (Gerald Murphy). This way Fitzgerald became the man that he admired and lived the heightened life that so appealed to him. Fitzgerald, in other words, created a larger world in his early drafts of the novel, and then he invited himself into this world, fulfilling in his imagination what he could not fulfill in life. Fitzgerald, however, saw himself in double context—as both success and failure—and he fused to Seth Piper's charm Francis Melarky's destructive nature. Here Fitzgerald was again using the irony that he so brilliantly developed in *The Great Gatsby*; but instead of the irony being completely a matter of point of view, he made it a matter of characterization —the ambivalence being not in the way Dick Diver is *seen* but in the way he *acts*.

Also, in the early draft, the Pipers have a dinner party, then there is the duel, and finally Francis accompanies the Pipers to see Abe Grant off to America. In *Tender Is the Night*, Rosemary becomes Francis Melarky, attending the dinner party, watching the duel, and accompanying the Divers and Norths to Paris. Fitzgerald, in other words, allowed Rosemary to stand for himself. Rosemary, whose most famous movie was called *Daddy's Girl*, is the very spirit of youth and success. She symbolizes a state of being that both Abe North and Dick Diver have known and lost. Abe North, at one point in the novel, is "happy to live in the past. The drink made past happy things contemporary with the present, as if they were still going on, contemporary even with the future as if they were about to happen again" [103]. Rosemary is the personification of this feeling—just as Ginevra King must have been the personification of this feeling for Fitzgerald. Ginevra kept the "illusion perfect," Fitzgerald once wrote; [10] and in a Josephine story ("A Nice Quiet Place," written at a time when Fitzgerald was working on *Tender Is the Night*) [11] Josephine, who is modelled on Ginevra King, is at one point mysteriously called Rosemary, a mistake that neither Fitzgerald nor his editor caught when the story was included in *Taps at Reveille*.[12]

Rosemary gives excitement to life, keeps the world alive, the bloom on the rose. Her beauty is something inviolable, something to be longed after. Fitzgerald could not live without this double focus—back toward the glory that was, forward toward the promise that might be, although the future seemed bleak in *Tender Is the Night*. If Dick Diver represents what Fitzgerald thought that he might *become*, Rosemary represents the spirit of what he once *was*. At the beginning of the novel, Dick feels that he holds Rosemary in trust, that he must guard her like a father protects a child [cf. 21]. At the end, as his decline becomes more serious, he seduces her. The seduction stands in contrast to an earlier scene, one that took place at the height of Dick's career, when Rosemary asks Dick to be her lover and he refuses. When he gives in, Dick loses his sense of wonder, he loses a point of view—a way of looking at life—just as Gatsby loses a point of view when he loses Daisy. Fitzgerald associated the theme of wasted youth and of failure in *Tender Is the Night* with child seduction. At his lowest ebb, under arrest in Rome, Dick says, " 'I want to make a speech . . . I want to explain to these people how I raped a five-year-old girl' " [235]. When Dick seduces Rosemary, he betrays a trust, just as Dick Diver and Fitzgerald himself believed that they had betrayed their own youthful talent, were reckless with time's promises, and taken too many wrong paths. Fitzgerald once wrote to his own daughter, "What little I've accomplished has been by the most laborious and uphill work, and I wish now I'd *never* relaxed or looked back —but said at the end of *The Great Gatsby* 'I've found my line—from now on this comes first. This is my immediate duty—without this I am nothing.' " [13]

Fitzgerald did not begin the Dick Diver version of the novel until after Zelda's breakdown in April of 1930. Certainly Fitzgerald felt that his marriage to Zelda had taken its toll on his energy. He wrote to his daughter in 1938 that when he was young he "lived with a great dream." Zelda hindered his ambitions because she wanted him "to work too much for *her* and not enough for my dream." Zelda "was spoiled," Fitzgerald said, "and meant no good to me." When Zelda broke, Fitzgerald continues: "It was too late also for me to recoup the damage. I had spent most of my resources, spiritual and material, on her, but I struggled on for five years till my health collapsed, and all I cared about was drink and forgetting." [14]

Fitzgerald obviously brought this emotion to *Tender Is the Night,* making Nicole into the spirit of Zelda, who drains Dick Diver of strength and energy. This is also what Fitzgerald must have had in mind when he wrote Edmund Wilson that he thought of Dick Diver as an "homme épuisé." [15]

Fitzgerald, however, complicated his own relationship with Zelda by making Dick the victim of the very rich. Here we are back with a Gatsby theme—in fact, the Warrens, like the Buchanans, are a wealthy Chicago family. Fitzgerald was once again venting his rage at people like Charles King and his family—or so the evidence suggests. At one point in the first edition of *Tender Is the Night,* Fitzgerald names Nicole's father Devereux Warren [166] and at another point he calls him Charles [320]. Bruccoli quotes a young writer, Charles Marquis Warren, who believed that Fitzgerald was using his name "as a friendly gesture." How one can so interpret being named after Nicole's father—a liar, a coward, a man guilty of incest—is difficult to understand. A more likely interpretation is that Charles (Devereux) Warren is a cruel distortion of Charles King—a fantasy projection of Fitzgerald's hurt feelings and his lively imagination. In this connection, it is interesting that Fitzgerald, in an early draft, named one of Dick's children Ginevra—and that he makes, in the final version, Tommy Barban, an unsympathetic character, a broker as well as a soldier of fortune [cf. 274.] The invention of Baby Warren may be purely mechanical (she develops out of Charlotte Melarky, Francis' mother). Fitzgerald needed somebody to embody the ruthless spirit of the very rich, get the upper hand of Dick, reject him once he served his purpose. And yet she reveals Fitzgerald's attitude toward the rich, embodies his bitterness. "I have never been able to forgive the rich for being rich," Fitzgerald once wrote, "and it has colored my entire life and works." [16] Fitzgerald also said that he took things hard, specifying his loss of Ginevra.[17] This particular incident in his life seems most responsible for his attitude toward the very rich, most responsible for the unsympathetic Chicago families of wealth that appear in his best fiction.

If Fitzgerald took Zelda's sickness as a starting point and coupled the drain of this illness upon him with his feelings toward the very rich, he did not make Dick Diver merely the victim of Nicole and her wealthy family. Dick is complicit in his decline. He is the "spoiled priest" as Fitzgerald refers to him in his plans for the novel. One of the most astute critics of this novel, Matthew Bruccoli, believes the two views of Dick—the "homme épuisé" and the "spoiled priest"—are somewhat contradictory, but this is because he misreads what Fitzgerald means by "spoiled priest" and does not fully see Dick's dual nature—that he is *used* by others because he *allows* himself to be used and is responsible in part for his failure. A priest is a man who has dedicated himself to a heightened purpose in life with a serious sense of duty. The "spoiled priest" has betrayed that sense of duty, lost self-discipline, and given way to excesses. In his Notebook, Fitzgerald once said of himself that "strict self-discipline" was "the secret of his charm": "When you let that balance become disturbed, don't you become just another victim of self-indulgence?—breaking down the solid things around you and, moreover, making yourself terribly vulnerable?" [18]

The dream in Fitzgerald's fiction is betrayed from within and without. From without it hits upon the rocks of crass materialism, flounders in contact with people (the Buchanans and the Warrens) hardened by wealth and their innate superiority. From within the dream is betrayed by misjudgment and self-indulgence. Gatsby misjudges the Buchanans, Dick misjudges Nicole's influence on him, and it is an interesting coincidence that Tommy Barban's words to Dick are exactly Gatsby's words to Tom Buchanan: "Your wife does not love you," said Tommy [Barban] suddenly. "She loves me." [308]. "Your wife doesn't love you," said Gatsby. ". . . She loves me." [131]. Gatsby indulges his fantasy beliefs that he can win Daisy back with a gaudy yellow car and swindler's money. Dick Diver's self-indulgence is more physical; the good life —the life of leisure and elegance—lures him to a point where the man of discipline in him is smothered. The "carelessness" of the Warrens has to be taken in context with Dick's carelessness toward himself.

Dick's main flaw is his desire to be loved and to be the center of attention. Both Fitzgerald and Dick Diver liked to feel people dependent upon them. Fitzgerald once said of himself: "I must be loved. I tip heavily to be loved. I have so many faults that I must be approved of in other ways." [19] Dick also is the victim of his vanity, and throughout the novel he goes out of his way to help others (a girl on a battlefield cemetery who is trying to put a wreath on her brother's grave, a girl and her mother aboard an ocean-liner, Mary Willis who shot down a man at the train station, a troubled girl with an extreme case of eczema). Fitzgerald suggests that it is his desire to help Nicole that leads to their marriage. He liked to give lavishly of his strength, cater to egos, and his vanity made him vulnerable. At the very end of the novel, Nicole tells Baby Warren, her hard-hearted sister, " 'Dick was a good husband to me for six years. . . . All that time I never suffered a minute's pain because of him, and he always did his best never to let anything hurt me.' " Her sister replies, " 'That's what he was educated for' " [312]. This is the thankless rich speaking, but Dick played into their hands. Dick's desire to be needed remains with him to the end. Even as Nicole is about to discard him, Dick answers the call for help from Mary North and Lady Caroline:

> "Use me!" [he says, hanging up the phone.] He would have to go fix this thing that he didn't care a damn about, because it had early become a habit to be loved. . . . Wanting above all to be brave and kind, he had wanted, even more than that, to be loved. So it had been. [302]

When Dick falls in love with Rosemary—who represents "all the immaturity of the race" [69]—he is already used up, and this scene reveals how completely he has abandoned his self-discipline, a discipline that has obviously been open to attack from the beginning. Although Dick is thirty-three years old when he falls in love with Rosemary, Fitzgerald portrays him acting as self-indulgently and irresponsibly as an adolescent. He waits for Rosemary at the studio, for example, "with the fatuousness of one of Tarkington's adolescents" [91]. He tries to becloud the fact that Rosemary is so young, and when he first kisses her, "her youth vanish[ed] as she passed inside the focus of his eyes and he kissed her breathlessly as if she were any age at all" [63]. Just before Dick consummates his love affair with Rosemary, his father dies. Dick has been brought up by his father to believe in the old virtues—" 'good instincts,' honor, courtesy, and courage" [204]—and his father's death symbolically parallels his own loss of authority and self-discipline. Furthermore, when Nicole falls in love with Dick, he takes the place of her father. The fact that she falls out of love with him and that Dick commits symbolic incest with Rosemary, an act which leagues him with Devereux Warren, reveals Dick's failure to become a responsible "father," a position which, in this novel, Fitzgerald seems to equate with maturity. Like Fitzgerald's earlier works, *Tender Is the Night* reveals not only a sense of regret for a past lost, but of regret for a future unfulfilled because it was irresponsibly wasted. Whereas a novel such as *The Great Gatsby* emphasizes the attempt to recapture the lost past, *Tender Is the Night* emphasizes the future that remained unfulfilled. Like Gatsby, Dick Diver felt that youth was something that could be drawn upon forever. But unlike Gatsby, he had the means, the talent, to make the dream come true. Dick is the victim of his own weak will.

If Amory Blaine wonders if the race is worth while, if Anthony Patch does not know when to begin running, if Jay Gatsby does not know when to stop running, Dick Diver does not know that the race is lost. When Tommy Barban tells Dick that Nicole is leaving him, Fitzgerald describes at the same moment the Tour de France, the cross-country bicycle race. A "lone cyclist in a red jersey" first appears, "toiling intent and confident out of the westering sun," then fifty more followed "most of them indifferent and weary," and finally a light truck took up the rear carrying "the dupes of accident and defeat" [310]. Fitzgerald establishes an obvious parallel between the descriptive detail and Dick's fate. Dick, who was once very much like the lone cyclist in the red jersey, is no longer even weary and indifferent but a "dupe" of defeat. When Dick first meets Baby Warren in the

Alps, he is on a bicycle trip [cf. 147–57], and when Baby Warren "dismisses" him, she remarks: " 'We should have let him confine himself to his bicycle excursions' " [312]. One of the last pieces of news about Dick from New York is that "he bicycled a lot" [314].

Dick Diver is like Anthony Patch in many ways: he is young and handsome, he likes to be the center of attention and to give himself lavishly to others, and he is essentially a weak and passive man. But where Anthony has only the hope of his grandfather's money to sustain him, Dick has committed himself to the study of psychiatry and has the promise of a brilliant career before him. The novel's thirteen-year span takes Dick from the age of twenty-six, when he is working his way to the top of his profession, to the age of thirty-nine, when he has given up the profession and given way to alcoholism and complete self-abandonment. As in *The Beautiful and Damned*, Dick has first the sense of promise and expectancy (here his hope of becoming a brilliant psychiatrist); this sense of expectancy lasts during the days and evenings of wild and riotous parties; this eventually gives way to a sense of waste; and the sense of waste is replaced by the regret that the time of youth has not been better used.

The theme of *Tender Is the Night*, in part, will be the theme of "The Crack-Up" articles, and two years later Fitzgerald will tell us that he lived

> distrusting the rich, yet working for money with which to share their mobility and the grace that some of them brought into their lives. During this time I had plenty of the usual horses shot out from under me—I remember some of their names—*Punctured Pride, Thwarted Expectation, Faithless, Show-off, Hard Hit, Never Again*. And after awhile I wasn't twenty-five, then not even thirty-five, and nothing was quite as good.[20]

Fitzgerald once said, "I am part of the break-up of the times." [21] He came to believe this in a literal way.

The Jazz Age, days of promise and gaiety, ended with the depression of 1929, and what Fitzgerald believed to be the pattern of human growth turned out to be the pattern of twentieth-century history. While accidental, it is nevertheless appropriate that as early as 1920 Fitzgerald thought that seventeen to thirty were the halcyon years. He had, of course, no way of knowing that what he felt to be a personal truth would become a historical fact when *The Great Gatsby* was published in 1925. But he did know it when he was writing *Tender Is the Night*, published in 1934, and it is thus significant that this story takes place—although not chronologically—between 1917 and 1930, and that it is about a brilliant young psychiatrist who in 1917 reveals great talent but who misused and dissipated it by 1930. As Dick Diver wasted his genius with riotous living and had only failure to show for it, so too, Fitzgerald came to feel, the riotous twenties led directly to the catastrophe of 1929 and the thirties. *Tender Is the Night* and "Babylon Revisited" clearly indicate that Fitzgerald believed in a one-to-one relationship between personal and historical tragedy and a causal connection between the irresponsibility that characterized the 1920's and the suffering of the 1930's. He thought of youth and of the gay twenties in exactly the same way —as a fixed quantity of time. In well-known passages from *The Crack-Up*, Fitzgerald's history of his personal demise, he talks about being "a mediocre caretaker of most of the things left in my hands, even of my talent," until one day he suddenly realized that he was involved in "an over-extension of the flank, a burning of the candle at both ends; a call upon physical resources that I did not command, like a man over-drawing at his bank." [22] As the Jazz Age drew too heavily on its financial resources, so Dick Diver drew carelessly on his emotional resources; and in both cases it led to bankruptcy—economic and personal bankruptcy.

In this context, Dick's desire to be loved becomes ironic. His contact with women throughout the novel tends to function within a father-daughter relationship, and almost all of the minor characters reveal the breakdown of natural love. *Tender Is the Night* is full of perversion and abnormal love: Campion, Dumphry, and Francisco are all homosexuals; Mr. Warren is guilty of incest; and Mary North and Lady Caroline turn out to be lesbians. Fitzgerald says that "it was as if for the remainder of [Dick's] life he was condemned to carry with him the egos of certain people, early met and early loved, and to be only as complete as they were complete themselves. There was some element of loneliness involved—so easy to be loved—so hard to love" [245]. *Tender Is the Night* is a novel about the failure of an individual—it is also a novel about the failure of society. In many ways, the world failed to come up to Dick's expectation of it. That is why the innocence of youth had such appeal for Dick, why he is so attracted to Rosemary, whose "fineness of character, her courage and steadfastness" stand in contrast to "the vulgarity of the world" [69]. When Dick violates her, he destroys his last image of innocence—of freshness, vitality, of promise and youth.

One of the novel's final ironies is that Nicole, who is twenty-four, can, thanks to Dick, salvage the remains of her youth—a time which she guards "jealously":

> She [Nicole] bathed and anointed herself and covered her body with a layer of powder, while her toes crunched another pile on a bath towel. She looked microscopically at the lines of her flanks, wondering how soon the fine, slim edifice would begin to sink squat and earthward. In about six years [that is, at thirty], but now I'll do—in fact I'll do as well as any one I know.
>
> She was not exaggerating. The only physical disparity between Nicole at present and the Nicole of five years

before was simply that she was no longer a young girl.
But she was enough ridden by the current youth
worship, the moving pictures with their myriad faces of
girl-children [cf. Rosemary], blandly represented as
carrying on the work and wisdom of the world, to feel a
jealousy of youth.

She put on the first ankle-length day dress that she
had owned for many years, and crossed herself rever-
ently with Chanel Sixteen. When Tommy drove up at
one o'clock she had made her person into the trimmest
of gardens.

How good to have things like this, to be worshipped
again, to pretend to have a mystery! [290–91]

Fitzgerald's careful choice of words — "anointed,"
"crossed herself," "worshipped," "powder" [cf. *Song
of Solomon*, 3:6], "garden" [cf. *Song of Solomon*,
4:12–14] — puts this whole passage in double context.
There is supposedly a religious quality to Nicole's
beauty and youth, and Dick, like Gatsby, becomes a
kind of sacrificial priest to the beauty and glamor of
the very rich. The deracinated people who form a
backdrop for the story of Dick Diver are very similar
to the characters in *The Waste Land*. The society is
sick, and these people corrupt and eventually sacrifice
their high priest. This is further suggested when Dick,
leaving for good the beach he had made popular,
"raised his right hand and with a papal cross he
blessed the beach from the high terrace" [314].

Fitzgerald often moved through metaphor from the
personal to the historical level. At one point, discuss-
ing Dick's lavish behavior, Fitzgerald said that "the
excitement . . . was inevitably followed by . . . [a]
form of melancholy":

The reaction came when he realized the waste and
extravagance involved. He sometimes looked back with
awe at the carnivals of affection he had given, as a
general might gaze upon a massacre he had ordered to
satisfy an impersonal blood lust. [27]

The reference to war is picked up in the novel as a
whole. Dick and Rosemary visit a cemetery for war

dead. Dick sees the First World War as bringing an end to class distinction, and he nostalgically regrets the death of the old order. This was "a love battle," he says, romanticizing the relationships that existed between the classes. "This was the last love battle" [57]. Fitzgerald had been reading Spengler ("I read him the same summer I was writing *The Great Gatsby* and I don't think I ever quite recovered from him"),[23] and he agreed with Spengler that each culture passes through a cycle similar to that of human life. Dick's decline parallels the decline of the West. He abandoned the old virtues of his father and dissipated his energies, just as western culture had abandoned the old aristocratic virtues for a crass materialism.

Fitzgerald believed that the turning point in America came after the Civil War. Grant, he says in *Tender Is the Night*, "invented mass butchery" [27]. Dick Diver is torn between allegiance to past and present as he thinks back on his father—a Southern sympathizer, who has told him stories of John Singleton Mosby and his guerrila band.[24] "The old loyalties and devotions" fought against "the whole new world in which he believed" [106]. Dick ultimately rejects his father's world, the aristocratic and "conscious good manners of the young Southerner." He "despised them because they were not a protest against how unpleasant selfishness was but against how unpleasant it looked" [194]. Yet the struggle between the two orders is real enough for Dick, who at two points in the novel [118 and 315] is connected directly with Grant's "destiny." A failure, his research days over, Dick's career, Fitzgerald tells us, "was bidding its time again like Grant in Galena" [315]. After an initial failure as an army officer, Grant returned to Galena, Illinois, from where he left a grocery store (Dick "became entangled with a girl who worked in a grocery store"), to fulfill in the Civil War a destiny that was to end one order and to establish another— that of the commercial and industrial interests—the new financiers. The story of U. S. Grant—the man who came back after a bitter defeat—seems to have touched Fitzgerald deeply. While he felt that Grant had been used by the new industrialists, just as Dick Diver had been used by the very rich, Grant's story also appealed to his romantic conviction that success, like the phoenix, can appear from the ashes of the past. In the holograph copy of *The Great Gatsby*, Jordan Baker asks about Gatsby's background and Nick mentions that nobodys often came "from the lower east side of Galena, Illinois." [ms. p. 55]

Dick's father died in New York state and was buried in Virginia. Dick brings the body South, and "only as the local train shambled into the low-forested clayland of Westmoreland County, did he feel once more identified with his surroundings" [204]. Fitzgerald could write these words with feeling because in 1931 his own father died in Minnesota and was buried in Maryland. And yet, like Grant leaving Galena, when Dick Diver takes leave of his father, he puts behind him an old and different way of life:

> Dick had no more ties here now and did not believe he would ever come back. He knelt on the hard soil. These dead, he knew them all, their weather-beaten faces with blue flashing eyes, the spare violent bodies, the souls made of new earth in the forest-heavy darkness of the seventeenth century.
> "Good-by, my father—good-by, all my fathers." (204–5)

Fitzgerald wrote these words out of his own feeling —in fact, he used in *Tender Is the Night* a passage from an unpublished (until 1951) paper that he wrote on the death of his own father:

"The Death of My Father"	Tender Is the Night
I loved my father—always deep in my subconscious I have referred judgments	Dick loved his father— again and again he referred judgments to what his fa-

back to him, [to] what he would have thought or done. . . . I was born several months after the sudden death of my two elder sisters and he felt what the effect of this would be on my mother, that he would be my only moral guide. . . . He came of tired stock with very little left of vitality and mental energy but he managed to raise a little for me. [25]

ther would probably have thought or done. Dick was born several months after the death of two young sisters and his father, guessing what would be the effect on Dick's mother, had saved him from a spoiling by becoming his moral guide. He was of tired stock yet he raised himself to that effort. [203]

Dick's father died in Buffalo, and Dick returned to Buffalo after his decline. Fitzgerald lived in Buffalo from the age of two to eleven, and it was here—when Mr. Fitzgerald was fired from Procter and Gamble—that he witnessed his father's cruelest defeat. The Fitzgerald family returned sadly and without success to the Midwest. Dick also is "without success" in Buffalo, and gradually disappears into upper-state New York. Fitzgerald, in *Tender Is the Night* as in *The Great Gatsby*, chose the details of his novels out of his own catalogue of emotional experience.

Fitzgerald, perhaps forcing the comparison, saw a strange parallel between the story of Dick Diver, himself, his own father, and Ulysses Grant. They were all men who knew two ways of life—who could look back on a glorious or a proud past, but who had been defeated in various ways by life. Behind the real world in a Fitzgerald novel is a golden one that is slowly vanishing from view, and Fitzgerald felt this was true in a general as well as individual way. Dick Diver's story is also the story of Grant, Fitzgerald's father, and Fitzgerald himself (note he named Dick's alter-ego Abe [Lincoln] Grant-North) as well as the story of Western civilization in decline.

Fitzgerald published one novel about deterioration

and decline in 1922 and another in 1934. *The Beautiful and Damned* is an inferior work because Fitzgerald was not fully in command of his craft, and because the matter of deterioration was not a lived experience. If *This Side of Paradise* was a form of preparation for *The Great Gatsby,* so *The Beautiful and Damned* was a kind of preparation for *Tender Is the Night.* The hurt that Fitzgerald experienced with Ginevra King and Zelda Sayre was badly embodied in *This Side of Paradise,* because it was not assimilated and because Fitzgerald handled it too literally—unwilling or unable to find imaginative ways of realizing the dramatic as well as symbolic quality of the experience. The fear of waste and decline that Fitzgerald depicted in *The Beautiful and Damned* was melodramatic because the ideas in the novel were unassimilated and because Fitzgerald was too intent on making Anthony embody the ennui of the smart set. Fitzgerald did not have to rely upon sophisticated clichés to write *Tender Is the Night:* by the thirites he knew firsthand—and all too well—the meaning of sickness, physical decline, and disappointment.

The short stories that Fitzgerald published between *The Great Gatsby* and *Tender Is the Night* reveal his change of mind and feeling, and they also give us a way to follow Fitzgerald's journey from one novel to his next.

In the March 1929 issue of the *Saturday Evening Post,* Fitzgerald published "The Last of the Belles," which has many of *The Great Gatsby* overtones. Told by a young man named Andy, the story occurs during World War I in Tarleton, Georgia, near an army camp. "It was a time," says the narrator, "of youth and war, and there was never so much love around." [26] Four young men are in love with one girl—Ailie Calhoun—the last of the belles. During Andy's first months at Tarleton, Bill Knowles disappears into the war, Horace Canby kills himself in a plane crash when Ailie refuses to marry him, and Ailie falls in love with

Earl Schoen. When Earl Schoen returns to Tarleton after the war, dressed so that "the background of mill-town dance halls and outing clubs flamed out at you" [268], Ailie breaks off their romance. At this point, Andy leaves to go back to Harvard, gets his law degree, eventually turns thirty, and returns to Tarleton in search of lost youth. There he proposes unsuccessfully to Ailie, and then has the taxi driver take him to his old army camp where he tries—also unsuccessfully—to recapture the romantic past. The tone at the end of this story parallels the tone of *The Great Gatsby*:

> The taxi driver regarded me indulgently while I stumbled here and there in the knee-deep underbrush, looking for my youth in a clapboard or a strip of roofing or a rusty tomato can. I tried to sight on a vaguely familiar clump of trees, but it was growing darker now and I couldn't be quite sure they were the right trees.
> . . . All I could be sure of was this place that had once been so full of life and effort was gone, as if it had never existed. [273–74]

When Andy loses the beautiful girl who embodies the spirit of the romantic past, he loses his youth and the sense of eternal promise which—in Earl Schoen's case—was betrayed by his lack of money. All the themes that are in *The Great Gatsby* are here—as well as the emotions of nostalgia and disappointment.

In the January and February 1926 issue of *Redbook*, Fitzgerald published "The Rich Boy," perhaps his finest short story. "The Rich Boy" is similar in several ways to *The Great Gatsby*. Like Gatsby, Anson Hunter has lost his first love, but he does not romanticize this loss; instead he feels that someone else must pay for his unhappiness and finds satisfaction in throwing over Dolly Karger and driving his aunt's lover to suicide. Others would have been added to this list if Paula Legendre—the only one to ever triumph over him—had not died in childbirth. Like Tom Buchanan, Anson Hunter is glib, hard-driving, hard-drinking, insensitive, and egotistical. He was born to believe that he is naturally superior. In fact, as the narrator tells us, he was never happy unless there were "women in the world who would spend their brightest, freshest rarest hours to nurse and protect that superiority he cherished in his heart." [27] Like Dick Diver, Anson is a born leader; people gravitate to him; and he is proud to be of service to them—in fact, it increases his sense of superiority. Yet, seen from another perspective, Anson—who feels that others exist for his comfort and who disposes of his aunt's lover and of Dolly Karger with ruthless dispatch—is a kind of brother to Baby Warren, and the theme of the ruthless rich establishes a bridge between *The Great Gatsby* and *Tender Is the Night*.

There are four short stories published between 1929 and 1931 which rehearse even more directly the general themes and situation of *Tender Is the Night*.

In the January 1930 issue of the *Saturday Evening Post*, Fitzgerald published "Two Wrongs." In this story, Bill McChesney, a successful Broadway producer, marries Emmy Pinkard, a young dancer from Delaney, South Carolina. Three years later McChesney has drunk himself to a point where he begins to dissipate his talent. Emmy gets stronger as he gets weaker—just like Dick Diver and Nicole—until he finds that he lacks the energy to do his work, that "he had come to lean, in a way, on Emmy's fine health and vitality." [28] In the end, McChesney is stricken with T.B. and goes off, alone, to a sanitarium in the West. Emmy remains in New York where she continues, with many signs of success, her ballet dancing— "the old dream inculcated by Miss Georgia Berriman Campbell of South Carolina [which] persisted as a bright avenue leading back to first youth and days of hope in New York" [240–41]. Emmy continues to look ahead with the expectancy of youth; McChesney has only the lost past to gaze upon. Quite obviously, there is a great deal in this story—physical breakdown, man and wife separated by sickness, the desire to realize the old dream by taking up a career as ballet dancer, the sense of lost promise, and the loneliness and the regret—which comes more or less directly from Fitzgerald's and Zelda's own experience, and which was to go into *Tender Is the Night*.

Another story which treats the theme of waste and deterioration is "One Trip Abroad," published in the October 1930 issue of the *Saturday Evening Post*. Nicole and Nelson Kelly, wealthy Americans, bring their youth and enthusiasm to Europe; tour North Africa, Italy, the Riviera, Paris, and Switzerland; and three and a half years later they have wrecked themselves with foolish living and self-indulgence. The story closes in a Switzerland sanitarium, where they are trying to regain their health, and where they see a rather unpleasant couple—unwholesome and dissipated—whom they met in North Africa. Suddenly they realize that these two embody the spirit of their own decline—that they are looking at an image in a mirror:

> "Did you see?" she cried in a whisper. "Did you see them?"
> "Yes!"
> "They're us! They're us! Don't you see?" [29]

Another story, "The Rough Crossing," published in the June 1929 issue of the *Saturday Evening Post*, also depicts an American couple, Adrian and Eva Smith, sailing for Europe. They act as badly as the Nelsons—both drink and argue and are jealous and suspicious of the other, Eva to the point of being suicidal. Fitzgerald adds to the story Betsy D'Amido who, like Rosemary Hoyt in *Tender Is the Night*, represents the spirit of youth and vitality. Betsy evokes in Adrian, at a time when he no longer thought it possible, the old excitement of youth—the feeling of new life, promise, and possibility: "Her youth seemed to flow into him, bearing him up into a delicate romantic ecstasy that transcended passion. He couldn't relinquish it; he had discovered something that he had thought was lost with his own youth forever." [30] When Nicole in "One Trip Abroad" has reached the lowest point of decline her jewels are stolen. When Eva reaches this point she throws her pearl necklace into the sea—and "with it went the fairest part of her life" [265]. Adrian also loses his sense of renewed youth when he departs from Betsy, who is being met by her fiancé. Yet, unlike *Tender Is the Night*, Adrian and Eva are together in the end—hoping to make a new start. Four years later Fitzgerald would know that this was impossible, and Dick Diver would slink—beaten, defeated, weak, and dissipated—into the limbo of upper-state New York.

"Babylon Revisited," published in a February 1931 issue of the *Saturday Evening Post*, is still another story that anticipates *Tender Is the Night*. In fact, as the following comparison shows, Fitzgerald even used passages from the story in the novel:

"*Babylon Revisited*"	*Tender Is the Night*
Outside, the fire-red, gas-blue, ghost-green signs shone smokily through tranquil rain. It was late afternoon and the streets were in movement; the *bistros* gleamed. . . . The Place de la Concorde moved by in pink majesty. [31]	. . . outside the taxi windows, the fire-red, gas-blue, ghost green signs began to shine smokily through tranquil rain. It was nearly six, the streets were in movement, the bistros gleamed, the Place de la Concorde moved by in pink majesty. [74]
He wasn't young any more, with a lot of nice thoughts and dreams to have by himself. [407]	He was not young any more with a lot of nice thoughts and dreams to have about himself. [311]

Like Dick Diver, Charles Wales has misspent the past, lived recklessly in Paris during the twenties, and s a pathetic figure as the story opens. His wife is dead; and his daughter, Honoria (the Murphy's daughter was named Honoria, but Fitzgerald seems to be punning on the name), has been legally adopted by his sister-in-law and her husband.

The story opens with the *ubi sunt* theme: " 'And where's Mr. Campbell?' Charlie asked" [382]. Mr. Campbell is gone—and so are most of his old friends. Charles Wales has Fitzgerald's characteristic longing to relive the past, to return anew to the days of youth: "he wanted to jump back a whole generation . . ." [387]. He is overwhelmed by a sense of guilt, feels that his past was a "most widely squandered sum" [388], and gives a street tramp a twenty-franc note in the hope that he can buy away this sense of guilt. But he cannot elude the past; it trails him in the form of Duncan Schaeffer, a friend from college, and Lorraine Quarrles, a worn-out beauty of thirty—both described as "ghosts out of the past" [390]—who try to get Charles to repeat the lavish time of three years ago and who cause him to lose his daughter just when Marion Peters was on the verge of relinquishing Honoria. The past still has its toll on the present. The story closes, as it opens, at the Ritz bar, Charles pondering his own life in terms of the Crash of 1929.

Fitzgerald has here set up an equation between personal and public tragedy. Time is thought of in moral terms. As the financial recklessness of the twenties led to the Great Crash, so did Charlie's reckless living lead to his physical and emotional breakdown, the loss of Honoria (his honor), and his feeling of regret and guilt about his misspent past. In the climactic scene, Charles accompanies Lorraine Quarrles and Duncan Schaeffer to the door; and when he goes back to the Peters' salon, "Lincoln was swinging Honoria back and forth like a pendulum from side to side" [404]. The pendulum is an obvious symbol of time; Charles is the victim of his past; and "Babylon Revisited" reveals—as much as any other

story—that Fitzgerald believed that time is given to u
in trust. The past lies about Charles Wales like ashes
and, because he is no longer "young," he has n
dreams to buoy up the future. At the very end of th
story, Charles asks the waiter " 'What do I ow
you?' " There are, of course, two meanings intended
here—one literal, the other metaphorical. Fitzgeral
often equated time and money, and Charles mus
continue to pay for time misappropriated—to pa
with his youth: "He wasn't young any more," Fitzger
ald will use the same words to describe Dick Diver
"with a lot of nice thoughts and dreams to have by
himself" [407]. Like Dick Diver, Charles stands
trapped in time—between the unfulfilled past and the
hopeless future.

The stories that Fitzgerald published after *The
Great Gatsby* contain all the elements of *Tender I*
the Night. "One Trip Abroad" is a study of physical
and moral decline; "Two Wrongs" is a study in
physical and emotional transference—the woman getting stronger as the man gets weaker; "The Rough
Crossing" is a study of deterioration—the process
made more pathetic because it is seen in contrast to
the vitality of a beautiful young girl; and "Babylon
Revisited" is a study in misspent time—the moral
consequences of Charles Wales's life being extended
to parallel the economic decline of the thirties. To
these stories, Fitzgerald added "The Rich Boy," and
related Dick's decline to the habit of mind of the very
rich with their sense of superiority and ownership.

Despite the fact that *Tender Is the Night* is built
up from the short stories, and despite the many
revisions that it went through, Fitzgerald never had
this novel under control, and it gave him the utmost
technical difficulty. Perhaps, as the above study suggests, he brought too many disparate elements to the
novel and extended the theme too broadly beyond the
story of Dick Diver to include American history and
Spengler's theory of the declining West. Whatever

may be the cause, Fitzgerald never really succeeded in working out a coherent and sustained point of view; was never satisfied with the inverted time sequence; and inserted a number of implausible episodes—especially the duel between McKisco and Tommy Barban, and the mysterious murder of a Negro on Rosemary's hotel bed. One has a feeling that Fitzgerald was overreaching in this novel, trying to make the sensational believable, and never quite succeeding. Certainly he does not have the control here that he revealed in *The Great Gatsby*. The language itself gives Fitzgerald away; there are too many passages like the following—vague and badly written—in which the reader does not know what Fitzgerald is trying to say:

> To resume Rosemary's point of view it should be said that, under the spell of the climb to Tarmes and the fresher air, she and her mother looked about appreciatively. Just as the personal qualities of extraordinary people can make themselves plain in an unaccustomed change of expression, so the intensely calculated perfection of Villa Diana transpired all at once through such minute failures as the chance apparition of a maid in the background or the perversity of a cork. While the first guests arrived bringing with them the excitement of the night, the domestic activity of the day receded past them gently, symbolized by the Diver children and their governess still at supper on the terrace. [28]

Passages like this blur the clean narrative line of *Tender Is the Night*. Fitzgerald, as everyone knows, thought of revising the novel by beginning with Dick's first meeting Nicole and proceeding chronologically. The source of unity in the original novel stems from comparison and contrast. We open and close on the beach, and the man we first see is endowed with the strength of youth and the sense of life's promise. This contrasts with the debilitated man at the end who is overwhelmed by his sense of waste. Fitzgerald thought a chronological structure might better show the cause-and-effect relationship of Dick Diver's decline. He most certainly is wrong in this conclusion, because he gave far more emphasis to the *fact* of Dick's decline, which supplies the emotional tone of the novel, than he did to the *reasons* for his decline, which are unclearly entangled in Fitzgerald's concern over Zelda's breakdown, his attitude toward the rich, and his own sense of lost vitality and promise. Fitzgerald's attitude toward Dick is the same personal and emotional attitude that he took toward all his characters; *Tender Is the Night* is not a clinical study of deterioration; and critics—Wayne Booth, for example—miss the point when they suggest that a chronological revision would bring out more clearly the central conflict of the novel.[32]

Whereas *The Great Gatsby* was a novel about what could never be, *Tender Is the Night* is a novel about what could have been. Dick Diver had the talent and genius to succeed; he also had in his youth the necessary vision and sense of commitment. He was sidetracked by the very rich and by his own weakness, which was to feel needed and be the center of attention. Both Gatsby and Dick Diver believed that they could make time stand still; Gatsby thought he could recapture the lost past, and Dick Diver thought that his future would wait for him. Fitzgerald suggests that both were not aware of the nature of time.

The title *Tender Is the Night* comes from Keats's "Ode to a Nightingale," where the speaker longs for a state of eternality while recognizing that he is subject to a state of temporality—a state "where youth grows pale, and specter-thin, and dies." Like Keats, Fitzgerald longed for a world of arrested time where love will be "Forever warm and still to be enjoyed, / Forever panting and forever young." But like Keats, Fitzgerald also knew that no such world was possible for men. Jay Gatsby was never able to learn this, and Dick Diver learned it too late.

COUNT OF DARKNESS
THE LAST TYCOON,
AND THE PAT HOBBY STORIES

IN OCTOBER, 1934, Fitzgerald published in *Redbook* a story about a medieval count, entitled "In the Darkest Hour." In April of 1935, he wrote Maxwell Perkins "that I've now made a careful plan of the medieval novel as a whole (tentatively called *Philippe, Count of Darkness—confidential*) including the planning of the parts which I can sell and the parts which I can't. I think you could publish it either late in the spring of '36 or early in the fall of the same year. . . . It will run about 90,000 words and will be a novel in every sense with the episode unrecognizable as such." [1]

Fitzgerald kept working on this project, and the second and third installments in *Redbook* appeared in June ("The Count of Darkness") and August ("The Kingdom in the Dark") of 1935. He never abandoned this project, although his plan for the novel changed and he did little work on it after 1935. In January of 1939, for example, he wrote Perkins: "*Philippe* interests me. I am afraid, though, it would have to be supported by something more substantial. I would have to write 10,000 or 15,000 more words on it to make it as big a book as Gatsby [which was about 50,000 words] and I'm not at all sure that it would have *great* unity. You will remember that the plan in the beginning was tremendously ambitious—there was to have been Philippe as a young man founding his fortunes—Philippe as a middle-aged man partici-

pating in the Capetian founding of France as a nation
—Philippe as an old man and the consolidation of the
feudal system. It was to have covered a span of about
sixty years from 880 A.D. to 950. The research required
for the second two parts would be quite tremendous
and the book would have been (or would be) a piece
of great self-indulgence, though I admit self-indulgence often pays unexpected dividends." [2] Eleven
months after his death, in November of 1941, *Redbook* published the fourth installment, "Gods of
Darkness."

Fitzgerald never went beyond the first phase of his
outline to Perkins, and the four parts of *Count of
Darkness* treat Philippe as a young man. The writing
here is perhaps Fitzgerald's worst, and it is difficult to
determine what he was trying to do and why he never
lost interest. The original plan indicates that he was
trying to relate the development of one man—his
youth, middle-age, and old age—to the development
of the feudal system, and he seems to be working even
more with the relationships between the personal and
the historical than he was in *Tender Is the Night*. The
first three *Redbook* issues depict Philippe embodying
the history of the Middle Ages. The time is 872, the
beginning of "the Dark Ages":

> One can think loosely of the Dark Ages as extending
> from the decline of Rome to the discovery of America
> [Fitzgerald writes]; but in the dead middle of those ten
> centuries, there were two hundred years so brutal, so
> ignorant, so savage, so dark, that little is known about
> them. It was the time when Europe was so overrun by
> the Northmen, Moors and Huns that it had fallen into
> a state of helpless and sub-bestial degradation. Leader-
> less, the wretched farmers had no protection from the
> fiercest hordes from the north and the east, or from the
> more skillful and better organized Saracens from the
> south. [3]

Philippe returns to the Valley of the Loire, "at a
point fifty miles west of the city of Tours," where he

claims this land in the name of his father, Count Charles, killed when Philippe was a baby by a Northman, Vizier, who took Philippe and his mother to Spain, controlled by the Moors. Philippe's mother eventually falls in love with Vizier and is content to stay in Spain, but Philippe, with his step-father's permission, returns to France, gets the peasants to revolt, defeats the Vikings, breaks with the Church, and sets out to reorganize Europe. When it is to his advantage, Philippe will cooperate with the King or the Church, but he is suspicious of both these forces, and a power struggle exists among them.

Fitzgerald seems originally to be depicting the common man rising under the leadership of a "modern" hero—idealistic yet practical, brutal yet sensitive, courageous yet cunning. Philippe, who speaks in modern slang and acts precipitantly, is almost a caricature of a Hemingway hero like Robert Jordan:

> "What is that you're cooking," [Phillippe asks Le Poire, who is ineptly leading the peasants when Philippe arrives.]
> "Who wants to know? Le Poire grumbled.
> Philippe stepped forward and slapped the man's face sharply.
> "Answer me like that once more, and I'll let the daylight through you." [4]

In the fourth *Redbook* installment, Philippe encounters a real threat to his new prosperity in the Duke of Maine. He kidnaps the Duke and threatens to kill him if the Duke's soldiers' attack. What follows is most puzzling. Griselda, Philippe's new love, and Jacques, his retainer, take him to a secret meeting—"the weekly Esbot of the Witch Cult"—and there he finds the main body of the Duke's forces. Becquette Le Poire, the daughter of the peasant Philippe so rudely handled, is the "chief witch," and she wants revenge against Philippe. Philippe threatens to have the Duke killed if he is not released, but Becquette refuses. Griselda then reveals that she is high priestess of this cult and releases Philippe, who is now aware that there is an evil power at work here, but that he must use it to save his country:

> I haven't got any conscience except for my country, and for those who live in it.
>
> All right—I'll use this cult—and maybe burn in hell forever after. But maybe Almighty Providence will understand.[5]

The intention here seems immediately political. Fitzgerald was writing this at a time when he saw the need of America to join with Russia in defeating Hitler, and he seems to be writing an allegory of modern history and not an allegory of medieval history.[6]

The intention also seems philosophical. Fitzgerald was still deeply impressed by Spengler. Spengler believed that there were three separate cycles of history, each about one thousand years in duration: the Graeco-Roman (Apollinian), the Arabic (Magian), and the European (Faustian). The Faustian or modern man cannot satisfy his unending desires, his excessive wants, his restless striving for something infinite. He also believed that the cycles of history paralleled the cycles of human life. Like Spengler's Faustian man, Fitzgerald's heroes have a sense of striving—an eternal sense of wonder and expectancy. In *Count of Darkness*, the course of history parallels the course of Philippe's life; the novel bridges the time between the Graeco-Roman and the European period; and we see at the outset of history the man of restless ambition.

Yet whatever Fitzgerald intended in *Count of Darkness* does not really deserve prolonged critical scrutiny because this novel is sadly inferior to his other writing and reveals how desperately he needed to write out of his own sense of experience. The value *Count of Darkness* does have is to reveal, in almost a grotesque way, that when Fitzgerald began work on *The Last Tycoon* he was thinking of history in personal terms. Fitzgerald never finished his personal history of the Middle Age—its development from youth to old age. He was also never to finish *The Last Tycoon*—his personal history of Hollywood.

In October of 1931, Fitzgerald went to Hollywood where he made $6,000 for five weeks' work at M-G-M. There he met Irving Thalberg, who had come to Hollywood in 1919 to assist Carl Laemmle at Universal Pictures and who, in the meantime, had worked his way to the very top of the industry. In 1937, Harold Ober, Fitzgerald's agent, got him another contract at $1,000 a week with M-G-M. Thalberg had died, at the age of thirty-seven, the year before; and Fitzgerald saw his death was a turning point for the industry. Thalberg, Fitzgerald believed, was an idealist in a materialistic world. The feud at M-G-M between Thalberg and Louis B. Mayer was for Fitzgerald a matter of principle—whether the movies were an art form, as Thalberg maintained, or merely a profitable industry, as Mayer insisted; whether Hollywood should be more concerned with quality films or with profit.

Since Fitzgerald had depicted in Gatsby and Dick Diver the idealist in a materialistic world, he could warm to the struggle between Thalberg and Mayer. He was also excited by the personal qualities of Thalberg—a man of energy, power, and decision who lived a heightened and glamorous life—and Thalberg became the model for Fitzgerald's Monroe Stahr.

Monroe Stahr came to Hollywood when he was only twenty-two and became an important and powerful producer long before thirty-four, his age when we first meet him in the novel. Fitzgerald hoped to portray in Stahr a man who had helped build a dynasty—who had created the world of movies—and then to show that world come tumbling down around him. Fitzgerald says in his notes: "I want to give an all-fireworks illumination of the intense passion in Stahr's soul, his love of life, his love for the great thing that he's built out here, his, perhaps not exactly, satisfaction, but his feeling of coming home to an empire of his own—an empire he has made. I want to contrast this sharply with the feeling of those who have merely gypped another person's empire away from them like the four great railroad kings of the coast." [7]

Just as Fitzgerald had first made Dick Diver into the image of Gerald Murphy and then turned Dick into himself, Fitzgerald made Monroe Stahr into the image of Thalberg and then fused this image with that of his own. Once again Fitzgerald created a heightened world and then invited himself in; once more he poured himself into the golden vessel of his imagination.

This method—starting with a heightened embodiment of self—had worked successfully in *The Great Gatsby* and in *Tender Is the Night*, but there is some doubt that it would have worked in *The Last Tycoon*. Monroe Stahr does not seem to be a consistent character. The man of integrity and character we meet at the beginning does not seem capable of the blackmail and murder he attempts, according to Fitzgerald's notes, at the end. He starts as Thalberg—with his energy, vitality, drive, and purpose—and ends as Fitzgerald—sick, frail, vacillating, and tired. At the beginning of the novel—as Stahr handles a board meeting, fires a director, criticizes the rushes—he is shrewd and decisive, makes accurate decisions, and is always in control. He is the source of unity, the emotional nucleus of the studio; he is the object of admiration, fear, and worship. At the end of the unfinished manuscript—as he talks with a Communist labor leader—he is loud and aggressive, boasts, misjudges his man, loses self-control, and makes a fool of himself. The transition from one man to the other is sudden and unjustified. Fitzgerald, in his notes, said that *The Last Tycoon* was not to be a novel about deterioration, but he seems to have made it one nevertheless—his own sense of reality affecting the way he depicted Stahr, although the tone of the novel never becomes as solemn as *Tender Is the Night*.

Fitzgerald once said that he "was a man divided." [8] If he portrayed his divided nature by having Gatsby *seen* in double focus and by having Dick Diver *act* ambivalently, he did the same in *The Last Tycoon* by creating, in the person of Wylie White, an antimask of Monroe Stahr. If Stahr embodies some aspects of Fitzgerald's life and character, Wylie White embodies others—just as Nick Carraway is Fitzgerald the realist looking at Gatsby, Fitzgerald the romantic. Wylie White, however, is not a central observer; and where Nick is drawn toward Gatsby in the course of the novel, Stahr and White become enemies. Wylie White, like Fitzgerald, is separated (actually divorced) from his wife, is cynical about Hollywood, and is unable to write scripts that satisfy the producers. When Fitzgerald went to Hollywood in 1931, he was assigned to the movie *Red-Headed Woman*, based on a novel by Katherine Brush, which was eventually abandoned because the heroine was made too coarse and unappealing. [9] Fitzgerald seems to have this in mind when Stahr, disappointed with one of his scripts, tells his writers, " 'We've got an hour and twenty-five minutes on the screen—you show a woman being unfaithful to a man for one-third of that time and you've given the impression that she's one-third whore' " [40]. Wylie White, like Fitzgerald, got the brunt of blame for the unacceptable script. Wylie is later also held responsible for a weak gangster scenario:

> "Who wrote the scene?" [Stahr] asked after a minute.
> "Wylie White."
> "Is he sober?"
> "Sure he is."

Stahr considered.

"Put about four writers on the scene tonight," he said. "See who we've got." [55]

Fitzgerald hated the way the studios assigned writers to work "behind" him (writing the same material independently) and the way his scripts were mercilessly cut. One of the biggest disappointments in his life was when Joseph Manckiewicz, a producer at M-G-M, rewrote the script of *Three Comrades*. "I am utterly miserable," he wrote Manckiewicz, "at seeing months of work and thought negated in one hasty week." [10]

Yet Wylie White, who seems to embody Fitzgerald's frustrations with Hollywood script writing, is not a wholly sympathetic character, and Fitzgerald's notes tell us that he betrays Stahr. Fitzgerald again seems to be putting his own experience in ironic context, writing against the grain of his own feeling by sympathizing with the Hollywood producer rather than the writer. Fitzgerald identified with both Stahr and Wylie White, and when he put them in opposition—seeing one as a kind of destructive complement to the other—he was again bifurcating his own dual nature, embodying both the mask and the antimask of that nature, seeing the writer in him destroyed and portraying the source of destruction. Wylie White sells out to the money grubbers. There is also a little of the writer *manqué* in Wylie. If the vital Monroe Stahr represents what Fitzgerald would have liked to become, Wylie White represents what Fitzgerald feared he would become. The final embodiment of this feeling is Pat Hobby—a pleasant drunkard, an inept cheat, a Hollywood failure; and Fitzgerald wrote against his own emotions—established an ironic distance between himself and his characters—when he made Wylie White unsympathetic and Pat Hobby pathetic.

The general structure of *The Last Tycoon* is similar to the business novels of Theodore Dreiser. We see

Stahr, as we see Frank Algernon Cowperwood, as both financial genius and lover—we move from the board room to the bedroom.

Sheilah Graham, as she tells us in *Beloved Infidel,* is the model for Kathleen Moore, the object of Stahr's love. With Zelda in a North Carolina institution, Sheilah Graham took her place in Fitzgerald's life, as Kathleen Moore takes the place of Minna, Stahr's deceased wife. Stahr, who loved his wife dearly, is attracted to Kathleen because she looks like Minna, just as Fitzgerald was attracted to Miss Graham who looked like Zelda—or so Miss Graham suggests. Fitzgerald first saw Miss Graham at Robert Benchley's party in the Garden of Allah; he left the party, and when he returned, he mistook her for Tala Birrell, in the same way that Stahr confuses Kathleen with her friend. Fitzgerald later met Miss Graham at a Writer's Guild dance, just as Stahr again meets Kathleen at a dance. Miss Graham ponders:

> . . . If I was Kathleen, Minna was Zelda. How much I must have reminded him of Zelda! Was this how I had appeared that night, when he stood at my door saying good-by, and I had not wanted to let him go and I had asked him in, and he had come in? Had he—has he—been reliving with me his life with Zelda? [11]

There are other similarities between Kathleen and Sheilah Graham: Kathleen is Irish but she lived, as did Miss Graham, in London; like Miss Graham, she was divorced from an older man who had befriended her; at the time that Stahr met Kathleen, she was engaged to be married again, as Miss Graham was engaged to be married when Fitzgerald first met her.

Fitzgerald was again writing deeply out of his own sense of experience, just as he had in *The Great Gatsby* and in *Tender Is the Night,* novels which so richly represented two facets of his life and character. Although these novels are very different from each other, they both depict the idealist in a materialistic environment—one from Fitzgerald's point of view of the visionary, the other from his point of view of the *homme épuisé*. Monroe Stahr is also the idealist in the materialistic world, and in many ways he is an incongruous combination of Gatsby's vitality and Dick Diver's world weariness.

In a letter to Scribner's, Fitzgerald said: "If one book could ever be like another, I should say it is more like *The Great Gatsby* than any other of my books. But I hope it will be entirely different—I hope it will be something new, arouse new emotions, perhaps even a new way of looking at certain phenomena." [141]. Certainly *The Last Tycoon* reveals that as a novelist Fitzgerald had "a new way of looking at certain phenomena." Monroe Stahr has realized his dream, and he seems to have few regrets. Unlike Gatsby, Monroe Stahr is shrewd and experienced, and he makes very few mistakes. Yet, like Gatsby, the past has a tremendous appeal for Stahr, and he carries with him the memories of his wife Minna and his growing love for Kathleen is, in part, an attempt to recapture the dead past—it is, in fact, almost an attempt to recapture his lost sense of youthful excitement and romance. Fitzgerald makes it brilliantly clear what the death of Minna took from Stahr's life:

> As Stahr walked back from the commissary, a hand waved at him from an open roadster. From the heads showing over the back he recognized a young actor and his girl, and watched them disappear through the gate, already part of the summer twilight. Little by little he was losing the feel of such things, until it seemed that Minna had taken their poignancy with her; his apprehension of splendor was fading so that presently the luxury of eternal mourning would depart. A childish association of Minna with the material heavens made him, when he reached his office, order out his roadster for the first time this year. The big limousine seemed heavy with remembered or exhausted sleep. [62]

Stahr realizes that Kathleen is his last hope—that his old and more vital point of view depends upon his marrying her. "This is your girl," he says of himself. "She can save you, she can worry you back to life." Like Dick Diver, Stahr needs to have people depend on him, and Kathleen "will take looking after and you will grow strong to do it" [115]. As Fitzgerald put all this in his notes, Kathleen "promises to give life back to [Stahr]" [151].

But Stahr does not marry Kathleen. In the incompleted manuscript, Stahr and Kathleen seem to drift away because of each other's inertia, their failure to be decisive. In the letter to Scribner's, however, Fitzgerald said that Stahr did not marry Kathleen because she failed to come up to what his imagination demanded of a woman. She was "poor, unfortunate, and tagged with a middle-class exterior which [did not] fit in with the grandeur Stahr demand[ed] of life" [140]. When Fitzgerald wrote this letter, he had intended naming Kathleen "Thalia" and, in time, he may very well have decided to change Stahr's motives as well as Thalia's name.

Whether or not this is true, it does suggest that, at one point in his thinking, Fitzgerald conceived of Monroe Stahr as a kind of successful Jay Gatsby—as someone who made decisions on the basis of imaginative ideals. And these ideals seem to be the product of a youthful vision. Fitzgerald makes this clear in the Scribner's letter: "Success came to [Stahr] young, at twenty-three, and left certain idealisms of his youth unscarred" [140]. This idea finds its way into the novel itself, and it is said that Stahr "had flown up very high to see, on strong wings, when he was young. And while he was up there he had looked on all the kingdoms, with the eyes that can stare straight into the sun" [20].[12]

Yet, like Icarus, Monroe crashes rudely to earth, not on waxed wings but in a transcontinental plane, and his death is a metaphorical conclusion of his moral and physical decline. As Dick Diver is sometimes seen from the point of view of Rosemary, so Monroe Stahr is seen through the youthful eyes of Cecilia Brady,

Fitzgerald's narrator, the nineteen-year-old daughter of William Brady, Stahr's rival. She has fallen in love with Stahr and admits that she had "the young illusion that most adventures are good" [11]. It comes as a shock for her to see Stahr humiliated by Brimmer, the Communist, who is trying to organize labor in the movie industry. Stahr considers himself a paternalistic employer, and it angers him to think that his workers would even want a union. This is the first defect that Cecilia has noticed in Stahr's armor and, in her embarrassment for Stahr, she wishes that he were ten years younger—not tired, worn-out, and the physically sick man she sees: "Suddenly I wished it had been about ten years ago—I would have been nine, Brimmer about eighteen and working his way through some mid-western college, and Stahr twenty-five, just having inherited the world and full of confidence and joy" [125–26]. Brimmer also looks at Stahr and speculates, " 'Is *this* all? This frail half-sick person holding up the whole thing' " [127]. One wonders how much Fitzgerald had himself in mind when Stahr's doctor thinks, "He was due to die very soon now. Within six months one could say definitely. What was the use of developing the cardiograms?" [108].

The seeds of promise growing in time to ruin is as much the theme of *The Last Tycoon* as it is the theme of Fitzgerald's earlier novels. Fitzgerald suggests this through allusion and descriptive detail. When Stahr first sees Kathleen, she is floating on the head of the Goddess Siva in a current of water released by a broken water main in the earthquake of 1935 [cf. 25]. Siva, in Hinduism, is the Destroyer, the destructive principle in life, in contrast to Vishnu, the Preserver. Stahr's destruction is contained in the very moment of promise, in the very hope for a new life. Throughout the novel Fitzgerald plays upon this theme. He says of Monroe and Kathleen: "They existed nowhere. His world seemed far away—she had no world at all except the idol's head, the half open door" [65, cf. also 81]. Later in the novel, Stahr and Kathleen watch from the beach in fascination as the grunion pile upon the shore intent on self-destruction [cf. 92].

Fitzgerald paralleled the destruction of Stahr with the destruction of Hollywood. He identified Stahr with the vital and romantic Hollywood of the past; and as Stahr declines there is the longing for the return of a golden age. In his letter to Scribner's, Fitzgerald said that he set *The Last Tycoon* "safely in a period of five years ago to obtain detachment, but now that Europe is tumbling about our ears this also seems to be for the best. It is an escape into a lavish, romantic past that perhaps will not come again into our time" [141]. "An escape into a lavish, romantic past": the theme here is the same as that of Fitzgerald's earlier fiction; only the perspective is different. Instead of putting the emphasis totally upon the loss of his hero's youth, the loss of illusion or of genius, Fitzgerald shifts the focus to a glamorous time and industry, an industry to which some of his most beautiful heroines aspired—Gloria Patch and Rosemary Hoyt, for example—and the decline takes place in the industry when it destroys its last tycoon.

In the synopsis of *The Last Tycoon*, put together from Fitzgerald's notes and from reports of persons with whom he discussed the novel, Edmund Wilson writes: "The split between the controllers of the movie industry, on the one hand, and the various groups of employers, on the other, is widening and leaving no place for real individualists of business like Stahr, whose successes are personal achievements and whose career has always been invested with a certain glamor. . . . In Hollywood he is 'the last tycoon'" [131]. And Cecilia says that Hollywood can be understood "only dimly and in flashes," that fewer than half a dozen men have ever put the puzzle together, and that "perhaps the closest a woman can come to the set-up is to try and understand one of those men" [3].

In telling Stahr's story, Fitzgerald was telling the story of an industry. And Fitzgerald associated the Hollywood that Stahr knew with beauty—and with youth. When Gloria Patch turns thirty, she is too old for Hollywood. And when Monroe Stahr dies, Hollywood loses some of its appeal—its glamor, romance, and sense of promise. It is taken over, according to Fitzgerald, by an ugly and unimaginative group. In a very real way, a least for Fitzgerald, Hollywood loses all the attributes he had predicated of youth.

Fitzgerald moves from the story of Monroe Stahr to the story of Hollywood, and in *The Last Tycoon* he spirals out once more and relates the story of Hollywood to that of America. At the very beginning of the novel, the Hollywood people visit at dawn the Hermitage, the home of Andrew Jackson, in a scene that has so many of the grotesque qualities of *The Great Gatsby*. Andrew Jackson, who opposed the national bank, was also, as the novel points out, the inventor of the spoils system—the man, in other words, who cancelled out his ideals. The Hermitage becomes a historical extension of Monroe Stahr's contradictory nature and of Hollywood where artistic integrity is corrupted by materialism—and it is symbolically proper that Manny Schwartz, once a success now a failure in Hollywood, should commit suicide there, as if it were the proper shrine [cf. 13].

Throughout *The Last Tycoon*, Fitzgerald makes the same kind of use of Abraham Lincoln, the man who comes at the moment of colossal transition in American history, as he did of Ulysses Grant in *Tender Is the Night*. With both Lincoln and Grant, or so Fitzgerald suggests, their ideals came to naught in a crass material and commercial world. Fitzgerald rather uniquely conveys this feeling when a prince, visiting the studio, sees Abe Lincoln "his legs crossed, his kindly face fixed on a forty cent dinner, including dessert, his shawl wrapped around him as if to protect himself from the erratic air cooling" [49]. If crass materialism was to profane the spirit of Lincoln, it was also to profane the spirit of Stahr because "Stahr like Lincoln was a leader carrying on a long war on many fronts; almost single-handed he had moved pictures sharply forward through a decade. . . . Stahr was an artist only, as Mr. Lincoln was a general." [106]

As in *The Great Gatsby* and *Tender Is the Night, The Last Tycoon* spirals out from a story of an individual to a story of history, from the personal to the public. The story of Monroe Stahr is the story of Hollywood—and, by implication, the story of America as well. Kathleen tells us that Spengler was a name on her "reading list" [cf. 91]. The reference is significant because as Monroe Stahr loses his vitality and goes into decline so also does Hollywood and America itself.

Most of Fitzgerald's short stories were collected to follow and take advantage of the sales of his novels. *Flappers and Philosophers* appeared in 1920 after *This Side of Paradise; Tales of the Jazz Age* in 1922 after *The Beautiful and Damned; All the Sad Young Men* in 1926 after *The Great Gatsby;* and *Taps at Reveille* in 1935 after *Tender Is the Night.*

"Crazy Sunday," a story about a Hollywood writer, was first published in 1932 and later included in *Taps at Reveille.* An interesting story, depicting the Sunday that Fitzgerald made a fool of himself at an elegant Hollywood party in Irving Thalberg's Malibu home, "Crazy Sunday" gains significance because it anticipates *The Pat Hobby Stories* which Fitzgerald began in September of 1939 and was working on at the time of his death in December of 1940. *Esquire* magazine began the series in January of 1940 and continued it for seventeen months—even after Fitzgerald's death —to May of 1941. Arnold Gingrich, who was then the editor of *Esquire,* has recently collected these seventeen stories and written an introduction explaining their publishing history.[13]

Fitzgerald was forty-three when he began these stories; Pat Hobby's age is forty-nine. Hobby is a tired Hollywood script writer, a success twenty years ago, but down at his heels in the stories. He is a kind of good-natured con-man who seldom gets away with his schemes to make a few dollars so that he can buy another pint of gin or spend the day at the Santa Anita race track. Hobby—a pathetic, clear-cut failure —is Fitzgerald's nightmare projection of what he might become in five or six years.

Most of the stories are very slight. Hobby tries— usually unsuccessfully—to blackmail a big producer; to steal another writer's plot or script (the basis of four stories); to keep an "extra" on the set, who is really an important writer in disguise, from sitting at the executives' table in the studio commissary; to pass as a friend of the big stars; and to impress a beauitful girl with his position in the movies. Hobby is not even a successful con-man, and he often is the one tricked or outwitted. Inept and fumbling, he will at times stumble across a stage and ruin a scene in a movie or, in another instance, ruin the whole movie itself.

The theme of age threads its way through these stories: "Pat Hobby's Christmas Wish" is the story of a secretary "about thirty-six, handsome, faded, tired, efficient" [2], who is transferred by an important producer—after eighteen years as his secretary—because, as she put it, " 'I depressed him—I reminded him he was getting on' " [3]. In "A Man in the Way," Pat steals the idea for a script: a poor old man tries to get a job as a laborer, crating and packing pictures, but he is not young enough. The old man, it turns out, actually painted the pictures many years ago. Pat likes the story, and enjoys telling it to the producers, because he could warm "to his conception of himself" [18].

A sense of a golden world lost pervades these stories; an age older and better has run out. Hobby's is the backward look—twenty years back, to the time when he ate at the executive table in the commissary, and to the years when he was on the way to thirty screen credits. He is excited only by the past, and when he boasts about his early years in the industry, "he felt young again, authoritative and active" [95]. In a story entitled "A Patriotic Short," Pat thinks back to the time he had lunch at the studio with the President of the United States. He was asked to take Doug Fairbanks' place so that the writers could be represented. This is the high point in Hobby's career, and he often wanders nostalgically back to the scene in his memory: "His memory of the luncheon was palpitant with glamor. The Great Man had asked some questions about pictures and had told a joke and Pat laughed with the others—all of them solid men together—rich, happy and successful" [118].

Hobby was twenty-nine when he first came to Hollywood, and his career does not begin to slide until his mid-thirties. Fitzgerald is still using the pattern of the earlier stories and novels: Hobby's early years in Hollywood are marked by the promise of success; he has talent and vitality and looks to the future with a sense of expectancy; then he begins to drink and dissipate his talent; the vitality begins to wane; and then comes the turning point. After the turning point, there is only the backward view, the glamorous past, the promises that never came to be.

The conflict in Fitzgerald' fiction goes beyond the struggle with self or the struggle with others—goes even beyond the element of history—and Fitzgerald wrote novels and short stories about battles with the clock. The antagonist is time, and the conflict involves a struggle with reality itself. Amory Blaine and Anthony Patch cannot commit themselves to the possibilities of time; Gatsby cannot realize that he is already the victim of time; Dick Diver miscommits his genius and loses his time of opportunity; Pat Hobby longs for happier times; and Monroe Stahr also feels that he has lost something valuable in the rush of time. The reader of Fitzgerald's novels feels, as John Aldridge states it, "the end of the big party is always implicit in its beginning, the ugliness of age is always visible in the tender beauty of youth." [14] Fitzgerald, however, only half believed this; and his young characters never believed it; they felt as immortal as the gods —that they could soar. They were brought down to earth by their vulnerability to the very rich and by their self-indulgence—and they are filled with regret and long eternally to relive the days of their misspent youth.

Hope and despair, promise and disillusionment, faith in the future and nostalgia for the past—all of these elements are in Fitzgerald's major novels and stories, and all of them are intricately related to the way he thought of youth—and of lost youth.

LITERARY REPUTATION is a capricious and unpredictable phenomenon of history. There is no need to repeat the familiar story of Fitzgerald's posthumous rise to literary prominence. Edmund Wilson's edition of *The Crack-Up* in 1945 enkindled interest in Fitzgerald by revealing once again Fitzgerald's tormented and driven life, the "real dark night" of his soul where it was "always three o'clock in the morning." These essays, which embarrassed Ernest Hemingway and John Dos Passos when Fitzgerald first published them in *Esquire,* are heavy with self-pity, just as *Tender Is the Night* and (in a different sense) *The Great Gatsby* are also sentimentally solipsistic. The confessions of 1936 and 1937 were the same confessions of 1945, only time had changed the perspective, and what appeared slightly self-indulgent in life now appeared "tragic" in death. The critics who tell us that Fitzgerald is a "tragic" writer do so because Fitzgerald told them that his life was tragic and because they like to think of Fitzgerald that way. They were as easily fooled by Fitzgerald's Romantic stance as he was himself. Gatsby and Dick Diver know nothing of an Oedipus's *hubris,* nothing of his remorse, and nothing of his final self-understanding. The tragic vision involves more than nostalgia for the lost past and a sense of waste and regret for what might have been.

Fitzgerald was unable to go beyond the Romantic

vision because something in his own sense of experience brought him up short. Isidor Schneider's suggestion that Fitzgerald was a victim of the capitalistic system—that his desire for money and the good life corrupted him—is too simple a solution,[1] and John Berryman only varies this explanation when he insists that Fitzgerald suffered from a destructive kind of literary schizophrenia when he thought that he could write both popular and serious material at the same time.[2] Hemingway has perpetuated this myth in *A Moveable Feast* by telling us that Fitzgerald began all his stories seriously and then changed them to make them suitable for the popular magazines,[3] as if a "twist" in plot is the only difference between serious and popular writing.

If the problem is more complex than the audience for whom Fitzgerald was writing, it is also more complex than Fitzgerald's subject matter. In Fitzgerald's own lifetime, H. L. Mencken objected to the triviality of subject in *The Great Gatsby*,[4] and Edward Dahlberg repeated this sentiment in 1951 when he referred to Fitzgerald's novels as "peopleless," by which he meant that they are full of superficial people unjustifiably impressed with their own importance and sense of tragedy.[5] Fitzgerald begs the question when he answered Mencken's objection by saying, "But, my God! it was my material, and it was all I had to deal with." Subject matter and the use a writer makes of it are very different matters. One can agree that a novelist has a right to choose his own subject matter—his Jamesian *donnée*. Yet one can hold the novelist responsible for his inability to realize fully what was dramatically and psychologically inherent in that subject matter. Fitzgerald was unable to realize his material fully because he could only depict what he was emotionally able to accept.

It is not by accident that there is as much interest in Fitzgerald the man as there is in his novels. We seem to know the story of Zelda's breakdown better than the story of Dick Diver's fate. A second-rate novelist in America—Norman Mailer is a perfect example—attracts scores of readers who are more interested in him than in his fiction. Although Fitzgerald is a much better novelist than Mailer, his life is also of compelling interest, perhaps because there is a complexity in his life that is only partially realized in his fiction. Fitzgerald the man was not as innocent as Gatsby or Dick Diver, not so completely broken by life. What is most touching in the Ftizgerald story, in fact, is the ability of the man to go on—still dedicated to his craft—when he was sick, lonely, worn out, and hopelessly in debt. Fitzgerald was a much larger person than Dick Diver because he was not quite so much a superman at the beginning and not so much a broken idealist at the end. While Dick is left with nothing, Fitzgerald was still dedicated to his craft, and he came to Hollywood with a renewed sense of courage and purpose at a time when a weaker man would have given up.

Although Fitzgerald lived a heightened life, he so feared the drab that he Romanticized and heightened even further his own sense of experience, and he had a ready-made audience waiting and willing to participate vicariously in this experience. Fitzgerald embodied almost too perfectly the psyche of his own generation. Born of second generation Americans who were bitten by the bug of money and success, he grew up a block away from a great "robber baron" at a time when the aristocracy was being levelled and displaced throughout the world. Money, not just birth, was the new criterion of status, and Fitzgerald brought his awe of the rich to Princeton, to Long Island, to the Riviera, and even to Hollywood. If his father had not seemed so inadequate in this changing world, perhaps Fitzgerald himself would not have felt inadequate. The attitudes that Fitzgerald took toward his father are complex and very important to an understanding of his fiction—and only Henry Dan Piper has until now seen this. If Fitzgerald admired his father's gentlemanly virtues, he was also ashamed by his father's lack of success. It was not Edward Fitzgerald's fault that James J. Hill's mansion was at the other end of Summit Avenue, but Mr. Fitzgerald's attitude toward the Hills was typically American, and he granted the rich their *droit de seigneur*. It was not by accident that Fitzgerald went to private schools in the East before he went to Princeton; and it was not by accident that he spent the summers in places like Lake Forest. Although Fitzgerald eventually came to think of money as a means to greater mobility, to a more heightened kind of life, the fact remains that money became an important value in his scheme of things.

This is hardly a new or startling conclusion, for almost everyone who has written about Fitzgerald has pointed this out. Yet what the critics have not really seen is how this attitude of mind affected Fitzgerald's fiction—how it led over and over again to a reduction of narrative complexity, a simplistic formula that turned drama almost into melodramatic polarities. His own experiences had in a way led to this simplistic reduction. The boy who idolized money was also the boy who had been called to war, and the war, as Amory Blaine tells us, was associated with the old order, the monied world of fat and scheming profiteers under whose authority men died "for an old bitch gone in the teeth, for a botched civilization." The boy who idolized money was also the boy who had been rejected in love by the very rich. One experience was personal, the other abstract, but they complemented each other, and the bitterness of lost love was intensified by the clichés about lost cultural ideals. There was, to put this differently, a ready-made foe. Fascinated by wealth and money, Fitzgerald felt that it was unsophisticated—and he was also too hurt—to give such fascination open consent, and so instead he wrote against the grain of his emotions by condemning the old order (*This Side of Paradise*), by declaring the meaninglessness of life (*The Beautiful and Damned*), by making the rich hopelessly spoiled and irresponsible (*The Great Gatsby*), by making them ineffectual parasites who have lost the capacity to love (*Tender Is the Night*), and by having the materialist defeat the idealist (*The Last Tycoon*).

Fitzgerald found this view emotionally satisfying because it never forced him to examine or question the motives of his heroes. He can think of them—and of himself—as more sinned against than sinning. The very rich betray his heroes' sense of commitment—betray Amory's sense of history, challenge Anthony's faith in the beautiful, and destroy Gatsby and Dick Diver. Fitzgerald's image of lost youth is really an image of betrayed commitment, although the theme of lost youth in *This Side of Paradise* and *The Beautiful and Damned* is hidden, as I have tried to suggest, under "pseudo" themes. Fitzgerald's youth worship originated at Princeton with his reading of Keats, Swinburne, Dowson, Wilde, and Rupert Brooke, but what started off as a somewhat pretentious literary disposition became a bunker behind which Fitzgerald took emotional cover. Fitzgerald's persistent theme of lost youth is really the theme of lost opportunity—a failure of permanent achievement—and the object of achievement is the splendid life which only the very rich can afford. So the very rich are both the models of an idealized experience and the agents who prevent Fitzgerald's main characters from realizing that experience.

Thus Fitzgerald's own entangled motives belie the system of opposites in his novels. As I have tried to show, if Gatsby in many ways is a thematic opposite of the Buchanans, he is in other ways a grotesque extension, a cruel distortion of their life and social position. He never rejects their values—this is left for Nick Carraway to do—and Gatsby's moral supremacy seems to stem from his obsessive fidelity to a Romantic conception of himself. His desire for money, in other words, is supposedly not an *end* in itself but a *means* toward winning Daisy Fay, an explanation which is part true but which fails to take into account that James Gatz changed his name and modelled himself on Dan Cody-James J. Hill *before*—not after —he met Daisy. Gatsby is just as acquisitive as Tom Buchanan, and he is just as intent on having Daisy as Tom is on keeping her. Gatsby gave imaginative consent to the world of Tom Buchanan—just as Fitzgerald gave such consent to the world of Charles King—and the fact that Gatsby lacks taste and social knowledge—is an outsider—does not make this any less true. Fitzgerald was too blinded by his own experiences—his sense of hurt and bitterness toward the rich, his sympathy for the poor boy who is their victim—to see that he was moving his characters toward types. He was also unaware that while Gatsby and the Buchanans are thematically and structurally opposite, Gatsby accepts and not rejects their values, and in reality Gatsby and the Buchanans complement each other. The relationship between Gatsby and Tom Buchanan—the idealist and the materialist battling for a woman whose voice sounds like money— means one thing on the surface and another beneath the surface, one thing to the mind of Fitzgerald and another to his emotions; and this contradiction reveals how completely he was at odds with himself when he was writing this novel.

It is both curious and appropriate that when the Buchanans are dismissed the father suddenly and mysteriously appears—old Mr. Gatz, from the Midwest, the land of "innocence" to which Nick desperately desires to return—to tell us about Gatsby's Benjamin Franklin-schedule for his son's "success." There is, of course, a conscious irony here: Mr. Gatz is still faithful to the dream that destroyed his son. There is also an unconscious irony: the son and the father are in a sense "reconciled" through failure.

Nick returns home at the end of *The Great Gatsby*, and it is most appropriate that when he turns to speak his first words (the very first lines of the novel), they are the words of his father:

> In my younger and more vulnerable years my father gave me some advice that I've been turning over in my mind ever since.
> "Whenever you feel like criticizing any one," he told me, "just remember that all the people in this world haven't had the advantages that you've had."
> . . . Reserving judgments is a matter of infinite hope. I am still a little afraid of missing something if I forget that, as my father snobbishly suggested, and I snobbishly repeat, a sense of the fundamental decencies is parcelled out unequally at birth [1].

The Midwest houses the father who (like Nick's) embodies the old values, and who (like Mr. Gatz) gives consent to the myth of success. There is a pattern of journey and return in Fitzgerald's fiction. And as Fitzgerald wanted us to accept the difference between Gatsby and the Buchanans, he also wanted us to accept the difference between the innocent West and the corrupt East, a contrast that will not hold up—for the West is also the source of the Horatio Alger dream, a starting place, be it remembered, for both Gatsby and the Buchanans. Henry Dan Piper believes that it is the "values represented for Nick by the image of his father that have saved him from Gatsby's terrible mistake." [6] He maintains that Fitzgerald gave a consent to his own father's Catholicism and that Fitzgerald retained "the residual tradition of moral values represented by the advice given Nick by his father—without the sectarian dogma." [7] Piper, I believe, is absolutely right: Fitzgerald probably meant to suggest something like this at the end of *The Great Gatsby*. Yet such a resolution means next to nothing. For what exactly are the old values? How is the world supposed to stand at "moral attention," as Nick wants it? How is Nick really better

off in returning to the wholesale hardware business
that so depressed him before he went to New York? If
this is Fitzgerald's solution to Nick's moral predica-
ment, it is an unexamined solution. Is he really any
better off by rejecting the high bourgeois society of
the Buchanans for the low bourgeois society of his
father?

The ending of *The Great Gatsby* may be emotionally satisfying but it is fictional "cheating"—and
cheating in the most Romantic way. And the pattern
is not limited only to this novel. Fitzgerald's heroes
look forward to the East with excited expectation, and
it is the promised land for Gatsby, Nick, Basil Duke
Lee, Amory, and, of course, Fitzgerald himself.
When they fail, they return home—to the West—
engulfed in nostalgia and overcome with a sense of
waste and personal regret. The East-West juxtaposition functions directly in relation to Fitzgerald's twofold attitude toward time: the time of promise and
the moment of regret have their spatial counterparts
in the juxtaposition between East and West. This
kind of parallelism reveals the simplicity of Fitzgerald's thinking and the personal quality of his social
dictums. For Nick's return West does not reveal social
truths about America; Fitzgerald is not trying to
suggest something like Frederick Jackson Turner's
thesis about the frontier. The return to the West is
really a form of escape, a matter of Fitzgerald's own
nostalgia about his boyhood. When Nick goes home,
Fitzgerald is recalling his own sense of youth—the parties, the old friends, the trains happily crowded with
handsome prep-school and college students returning for Christmas vacation, perhaps even Fitzgerald's
own return home to finish his first novel after his
failure in New York advertising—and he fails to
consider the Midwest as a place of provincial con-
formity from which Nick had been trying to escape,
along with the many characters in the novels of
Sinclair Lewis, Sherwood Anderson, Glenway Wes-
cott, and Floyd Dell.

Nick's return to the Midwest was Fitzgerald's way of rejecting the Buchanans and New York—symbols of success and the hope of attainment—and of accepting Gatsby—symbol of failure and disappointment. Nick's return does not really resolve his dispute with the Buchanans; in fact, it is really an escape from having to cope with such people, a kind of emotional retreat to the world of the father. And it is important to note that both Nick and Gatsby "return"—either metaphorically or literally—to the father. In Fitzgerald's fiction, you cannot go home again—unless you failed—a fact that Fitzgerald was never able to understand or willing to examine, but one that he seems to have found emotionally satisfying.

The father or the ghost of the father haunts both *The Great Gatsby* and *Tender Is the Night*, and in both cases he is a good man who has led an undistinguished, somewhat pathetic life, virtuous—as in the case of Dick Diver—but a failure by American standards of success. This kind of man, modelled too closely on Edward Fitzgerald, Fitzgerald's own father, is counterpointed against another kind of father, a spiritual one like Father Darcy in *This Side of Paradise*, modelled on Monsignor Fay, Fitzgerald's close boyhood adviser and friend, whose esthetic values offer a substantial contrast to those of the materialistic culture. If there is any connection between the names Sigourney Fay and Daisy Fay, it is perhaps the suggestion, deep in Fitzgerald's mind,[8] that Daisy Fay embodied more than the dream, more than the pursuit of an ideal in a material world—an idea which is really a caricature of itself because Daisy is a fraud, a living testimony to the impossibility of Gatsby's dream in the first place. If one is willing to grant the possibility of this kind of unconscious connection in Fitzgerald's thinking, we can see how in Daisy it was also the father who betrayed the son and how the son remained faithful to the father—faithful to the disastrous end. This idea is not as farfetched as it may first seem. Fitzgerald was fascinated by *la belle dame sans merci*, the fair maiden who leads the hero to his destructive end, an end which in *Tender Is the Night* brings Dick Diver to the point where he feels a strange and sudden fidelity to his father. Daisy Fay is even more the *femme fatale* than Nicole Warren, and Gatsby's father is there to receive the fallen son after the ordeal. Fitzgerald and his heroes seem bent on failure—almost as if the peace of mind or the repose of the father's soul depended on it. In fact, the journey itself is a way for the Fitzgerald hero to act out the story of his father—the circular move that begins with the quest for success and ends with the reality of failure. The father comes to embody lost or desired ideals; the very rich embody qualities that are destructive to these ideals; the affinity of mind between the father and the rich is hidden under a blanket of prose; and the failure of the son becomes Fitzgerald's way of emotionally rejecting the world of wealth and of accepting the world of the father—another way, that is, of not having to admit failure and of not having to examine failure as a state of mind.

We can clearly see this pattern in *The Great Gatsby*. If Fitzgerald had accepted the Buchanans, he would have been accepting everything his father was not. If he rejected Gatsby, he would have been betraying the spirit of his father, the man whose idealism redeemed his lack of success (Fitzgerald referred to his own father's failure as his lost "immaculateness of purpose"). This duality led Fitzgerald to narrative extremes: the Buchanans are made brutal and ruthless—a caricature, as I have suggested of the King family—so that they can be more easily dismissed. And Gatsby is made into a Romantic idealist so that he can be affirmed.

We can see the pattern again in *Tender Is the Night*. The father and the Warrens represent two different versions of the past. The father embodies the "old virtues," the virtues of the Southern aristocracy,

The Warrens represent the corruption of those values, a corruption that in this case has led to the destruction of Dick Diver. There is in *Tender Is the Night* a sense of the son who has been cut off from the father ("good-by, my father—good-by, all my fathers") by forsaking the father's world and by betraying what the father stood for. When Dick Diver disappears into upper-state New York, he is in search of the father—a search which suggests that the father was not a failure after all and that his virtues are the ones that make life possible. And Dick Diver is really Fitzgerald himself in search of the father because upper-state New York was the scene of Edward Fitzgerald's failure with Procter and Gamble.

There is, of course, a confusion here, an idealizing of the father. Fitzgerald was unable to see that the Buchanans and the Warrens were a logical extension of his own father's world—of what his father would have liked to be—and that both Gatsby and Dick Diver were their father's sons in giving emotional consent to that world. To admit this would be to admit that the father, as well as Gatsby and Dick Diver, was an unredeemed failure. So the father is removed from the enemy's camp and made an adjunct of the Romantic vision, or made to stand for the old moral values which have been lost.

Fitzgerald's novels are studies in the fact, not the process of loss. Fitzgerald was unable to make his central characters responsible for their failure and defeat because he was too intent on justifying his characters and placing the blame on the very rich. Fitzgerald's novels beg very important questions by staging mock battles between the young idealist and the rich materialist who betrays him, never really showing that the idealist is really a frustrated materialist who bertays himself. The promises of youth are never fulfilled, and lost youth is always a matter of betrayed commitment. The loss of promise leads to flight—flight into the past, often in search of the father whose values have been unjustifiably idealized. The closest Fitzgerald came to depicting a hero who is the source of his own fate is in *Tender Is the Night* where there is something self-destructive in Dick Diver's consent to be used, his desire to be loved. But the Osiris quality of Dick's character as well as his self-destructiveness is never fully depicted, never brought into clear focus. The Warrens are made so brutally callous that in the end Dick becomes the priest, physically ruined but morally superior, blessing the hopeless people on the beach and going in search of the lost father whose spirit is as much on the beach as in upper-state New York. The novel opens and closes on the beach, and we have two contrasting portraits of Dick Diver—one in his prime, the other in his decline. Fitzgerald was only fooling himself in thinking that a chronological sequence would make Dick Diver's decline any more psychologically complex.

Fitzgerald could not depict the meaning of defeat as a state of mind because this would be to admit its causes were also a state of mind. He could convincingly portray the dream and the nostalgia for the lost past. But he could not render the aftermath of waste, the reality of failure, in any other terms but those of flight and self-pity. Nick Carraway and Dick Diver take flight. Charles Wales visits the old Paris and gives way to hopeless self-pity, just as Pat Hobby in Hollywood also feels sorry for himself. The fact that Fitzgerald believed, in *Tender Is the Night*, that the hero should fade away—believed, that is, in what he called "the dying fall"—only reveals that he was trying to find artistic justification for his inability to pursue Dick down the path of defeat.

One of Fitzgerald's main weaknesses as a novelist is that he could create a world that was emotionally but not logically satisfying, a fiction that came at times close to melodramatic stock situations. The best Fitzgerald could do with his experience was to depict it ironically, to show Nick Carraway attracted and repulsed at the same time. But this does not eliminate the dualities, and we still have the Buchanans at one extreme and Gatsby at the other. Fitzgerald would never endow Tom Buchanan with Gatsby's imagination—the idealist and the materialist always had to remain worlds apart. The moral polarities, the innocent hero, the betrayed commitment, the cruel waste of youth, the irreversible march of time, the Romantic flight, the lonely victim—these elements are Fitzgerald's narrative watermarks, irrefutable evidence that he took wanton satisfaction in self-pity.

Fitzgerald's self-pity forced him to write against the grain of his own experience. He knew first hand the materialistic quality of the dreamer, but to admit that Gatsby and Tom Buchanan were alike would be to make Gatsby pathetic with no redeeming virtues. So Fitzgerald circumscribed his narrative action, began his novel with the assumption that money corrupts, and reduced all moral questions to those polarity positions that he could emotionally accept. Fitzgerald rejected the "drab as subject matter." [9] He wrote so that he could bring into his life through fiction "a special emotion, a special experience." [10] He was too obsessed with avoiding the reality of failure to be fascinated with its psychological causes and complexities. His craft was a means of flight for him—into a brighter and better world where he could relive his hurts and where people would act as he could expect. Like Nick Carraway and Dick Diver, Fitzgerald longed to escape into a kind of boyhood world where the authority of the father would be a solace, a source of comfort in defeat, and in a very real way he found such an avenue of escape. For Fitzgerald escaped into his fiction—which became the most abiding and worthwhile escape of all—an escape which, in his case, led to truly permanent achievement.

1 — F. Scott Fitzgerald and the Romantic Tradition

1. T. E. Hulme, "Romanticism and Classicism," *Specula-tions: Essays of Humanism and the Philosophy of Art*, ed. Herbert Read (New York: Harcourt, Brace & Co., 1924); reprinted in *Criticism: The Major Texts*, ed. Walter J. Bate (New York: Harcourt, Brace & Co., 1952), p. 567.

2. Alex Comfort, *Art and Social Responsibility: Lectures in the Ideology of Romanticism* (London: The Falcon Press, 1946), p. 19.

3. Herbert Read, "Introduction," *Surrealism* (New York: Harcourt, Brace & Co., 1936), p. 90.

4. Hoxie N. Fairchild, *The Romantic Quest* (New York: Columbia University Press, 1931), p. 251.

5. Morse Peckham, "Toward a Theory of Romanticism," *PMLA*, LXVI (1951), 5–23.

6. F. Scott Fitzgerald, *This Side of Paradise* (New York: Charles Scribner's Sons, 1960), p. 17. All further quotations are from this edition, page reference indicated in brackets after the quote.

7. F. Scott Fitzgerald, *The Beautiful and Damned* (New York: Charles Scribner's Sons, 1922), p. 126. All further quotations are from this edition, page reference indicated in brackets after the quote.

8. F. Scott Fitzgerald, *The Great Gatsby* (New York: Charles Scribner's Sons, 1953), p. 2. All further quotations are from this edition, page reference indicated in brackets after the quote.

9. F. Scott Fitzgerald, *Tender Is the Night* (New York: Charles Scribner's Sons, 1934), pp. 115–17. All further quotations are from this edition, page reference indicated in brackets after the quote.

10. F. Scott Fitzgerald, *The Last Tycoon* (New York: Charles Scribner's Sons, 1941), p. 20. All further quotations

are from this edition, page reference indicated in brackets after the quote.

11. Hulme, p. 566.

12. *The Letters of F. Scott Fitzgerald,* ed. Andrew Turnbull (New York: Charles Scribner's Sons, 1963), p. 323.

13. *English Poetry and Prose of the Romantic Movement,* ed. George B. Woods (New York: Scott, Foresman & Co., 1950), p. 1357.

14. Cf. *The Letters,* p. 320.

15. Jean-Jacques Rousseau, *The Confessions of* (London: Penguin Books, 1953), p. 48. All further quotations are from this edition, page reference indicated in brackets after the quote.

16. George Noel Gordon, Lord Byron, *Childe Harold's Pilgrimage,* Canto III, Stanza 77, see Woods's *English Poetry and Prose of the Romantic Movement,* p. 561.

17. *The Letters,* p. 88.

18. *Ibid.,* p. 528.

19. Tristram P. Coffin, "Gatsby's Fairy Lover," *Midwest Folklore,* X, 2 (Summer, 1960), p. 83.

20. John Grube, *"Tender Is the Night:* Keats and Scott Fitzgerald," *The Dalhousie Review,* XLIV, 4 (Winter, 1964–65), 433–41.

21. Sheilah Graham and Gerold Frank, *Beloved Infidel* (New York: Bantam Books, 1959), pp. 195 and 198.

22. Henry Dan Piper, "Fitzgerald's Cult of Disillusion," *American Quarterly,* III, 1 (Spring, 1951), 69–80.

23. *This Side of Paradise,* p. 74. The poem can be found complete in *The Best of Swinburne,* eds. Clyde K. Hyder and Lewis Chase (New York: Thomas Nelson and Sons, 1937), p. 3. All further quotations are from this edition, page reference indicated in brackets after the quote.

24. Walter Pater, *Marius the Epicurean* (New York: The Modern Library, 1921), pp. 19 and 36. All further quotations are from this edition, page reference indicated in brackets after the quote.

25. Ernest Dowson, *The Poems of,* ed. Mark Longaker (Philadelphia: University of Pennsylvania Press, 1962), pp. 146–47. All further quotations are from this edition, page reference indicated in brackets after the quote.

26. Christopher Hassall, *Rupert Brooke* (London: Faber an Faber, 1964), p. 43.

27. *The Letters*, p. 317.

28. *Ibid.*, p. 414.

29. Rupert Brooke, *The Collected Poems of*, intro. by George E. Woodberry (New York: Dodd, Mead & Co., 1952), p. 43. All further quotations are from this edition, page reference indicated in brackets after the quote.

30. *The Letters*, pp. 323 and 469.

31. H. G. Wells, *Tono-Bungay*, intro. by Theodore Dreiser (New York: Duffield & Co., 1929), p. 117. All further quotations are from this edition, page reference indicated in brackets after the quote.

32. H. G. Wells, *The New Machiavelli* (New York: Duffield & Co., 1910), p. 385. All further quotations are from this edition, page reference indicated in brackets after the quote.

33. Oscar Wilde, *The Picture of Dorian Gray* (New York: Doubleday, Page & Co., 1923), pp. 46–47. All further quotations are from this edition, page reference indicated in brackets after the quote.

34. See James E. Miller, Jr., *The Fictional Technique of Scott Fitzgerald* (The Hague: Martinus Nijhoff, 1957), pp. 41 ff.; and William Goldhurst, *F. Scott Fitzgerald and his Contemporaries* (New York: World Publishing Co., 1963), pp. 74–104.

35. See also *This Side of Paradise*, p. 209 and *The Letters*, pp. 144 and 464.

36. Frank Norris, *Vandover and the Brute* (New York: Doubleday, Page & Co., 1914), p. 278.

37. Joseph Conrad, *Nigger of the "Narcissus"* (London: John Grant, 1925), p. viii.

38. Joseph Conrad, "Youth," *Youth: A Narrative and Two Other Stories* (London: John Grant, 1925), p. 42. All further quotations are from this edition, page reference indicated in brackets after the quote.

39. Joseph Conrad, *Victory* (London: John Grant, 1925), p. 410.

40. Joseph Conrad, "The Secret Sharer," *'Twixt Land and Sea'* (London: John Grant, 1925), p. 94. All further quotations are from this edition, page reference indicated in brackets after the quote.

41. Joseph Conrad, *The Shadow-Line: A Confession* (London: John Grant, 1925), p. 3. All further quotations are from

this edition, page reference indicated in brackets after the quote.

42. *The Letters*, pp. 289–90.

43. There is no book, to my knowledge, entitled *The Rise of the Colored Empires*. There is, however, a book entitled *Civilisation and Civilisations, An Essay on the Spenglerian Philosophy of History* by E. H. Goddard and P. A. Gibbons. Tom's description would nicely fit this book, but he could not have had it in mind because it was published by Boni and Liveright in 1926, a year after *The Great Gatsby*. Ernest Hope Goddard (1879–1939) was an assistant editor of *The Illustrated London News* and *The Sketch*. The *News* contained many articles on anthropology and archeology and was interested in the history of past civilizations. It is unlikely, however, that Fitzgerald had either E. H. Goddard or the *News* in mind when Tom talks about Goddard's book, but the similarity of names and subject is indeed a coincidence. The book that Tom more likely did have in mind is Lothrop Stoddard's *The Rising Tide of Color*, published by Charles Scribner's Sons in 1920. Stoddard believed that the colored races would eventually control the world. "Some four-fifths of the entire white race," he argued, "is concentrated on less than one-fifth of the white world's territorial area (Europe), while the remaining one-fifth of the race (some 110,000,000 souls), scattered to the end of the earth, must protect four-fifths of the white territorial heritage against the pressure of colored races eleven times its numerical strength" [p. 6]. In the holograph version of *The Great Gatsby*, the owl-eyed man picked from Gatsby's library shelf Volume one of Stoddard's *Lectures*, but Fitzgerald deleted this detail from the published version of *The Great Gatsby*.

44. *The Letters*, p. 462.

45. Ernest Hemingway, *A Farewell to Arms* (New York: Charles Scribner's Sons, 1929), p. 191. All further quotations are from this edition, page reference indicated in brackets after the quote.

46. Ernest Hemingway, *The Sun Also Rises* (New York: Charles Scribner's Sons, 1926), p. 10. All further quotations are from this edition, page reference indicated in brackets after the quote.

47. William Faulkner, "The Bear," *Go Down, Moses* (New York, Modern Library, 1955), pp. 218, 231, and 241.

2—*Irony and the Three Realms of Time*

1. "Author's House," *Esquire*, July, 1936; reprinted in *Afternoon of an Author*, ed. Arthur Mizener (Princeton, N. J.: Princeton University Library, 1957), pp. 185–86.

2. Fitzgerald's Notebooks; see *The Crack-Up*, ed. Edmund Wilson (New York: New Directions, 1956), p. 180. The Special Collection's Room at Princeton University has the two gray-colored loose-leaf notebooks which Fitzgerald used to record anecdotes, clippings, conversations overheard, descriptions, ideas, plot possibilities, and notes on present and projected writing. This material is arranged in alphabetical groups, and each section of the Notebooks has been tagged for easy reference. As Edmund Wilson suggests, Fitzgerald probably got his idea for the Notebooks from Samuel Butler, whom Fitzgerald admired from his college days. Wilson has republished large selections from the Notebooks in *The Crack-Up*, pp. 93–242.

3. "Early Success," *American Cavalcade*, October, 1937; reprinted in *The Crack-Up*, p. 89. Early success brought Fitzgerald handsome financial returns, and overnight he moved from a modest income to (in 1920) real wealth. Following is a record of his income from 1919 to 1936:

1919	$879.00	1928	$25,732.96 (including $1,000 from advertisers)
1920	$18,850.00		
1921	$19,065.18	1929	$32,448.18
1922	$25,135.00	1930	$33,090.10
1923	$28,759.78	1931	$37,599.00 (including $6,000 from M-G-M)
1924	$20,310.22		
1925	$18,333.61	1932	$15,823.40
1926	$25,686.05	1933	$16,328.03
1927	$29,737.87	1934	$20,032.33
		1935	$16,845.16 (paid tax on
		1936	$10,180.97 $17,153.13)

4. In a letter to Mrs. Richard Taylor, June 10, 1917; *The Letters of F. Scott Fitzgerald*, ed. Andrew Turnbull (New York: Charles Scribner's Sons, 1963), p. 414.

5. *The Nassau Literary Magazine*, May, 1917. These lines were originally published as poetry; Fitzgerald turned them

into prose and used them as the epilogue to Book I of *This Side of Paradise.*

6. "Princeton," *College Humor*, December, 1927; reprinted in *Afternoon of an Author*, p. 79.

7. Arthur Mizener, *The Far Side of Paradise* (Boston: Houghton Mifflin, 1951), p. 69.

8. Andrew Turnbull, *Scott Fitzgerald* (New York: Charles Scribner's Sons, 1962), p. 35.

9. Mizener, p. 79.

10. "My Lost City," *Esquire*, July, 1932; reprinted in *The Crack-Up*, p. 33.

11. *The Great Gatsby* (New York: Charles Scribner's Sons, 1953), p. 136.

12. *The Letters of F. Scott Fitzgerald*, ed. Andrew Turnbull (New York: Charles Scribner's Sons, 1963), p. 71.

13. Turnbull, p. 260.

14. *Ibid.*, p. 3.

15. Michael Mok, "The Other Side of Paradise," the New York *Post*, September 25, 1936.

16. *The Letters*, p. 393.

17. *Ibid.*, p. 193.

18. Fitzgerald's Ledger, p. 182; see Mizener, p. 210. Fitzgerald used a bookkeeper's ledger to record important events in his life, to keep a record of his published fiction (the date it was written, the company or the magazine which published or republished his work, and the date each story or novel appeared), and to record all money that he earned by writing since leaving the army (that is, from 1919) to 1936 (after which we still have the list of Fitzgerald's published works but not his royalties). The Ledger now belongs to Fitzgerald's daughter, Mrs. Frances Fitzgerald Lanahan, but the Princeton Special Collection's Room has a photographic copy of it.

19. "The Rough Crossing," *Saturday Evening Post*, June 8, 1929; reprinted in *The Stories of F. Scott Fitzgerald*, ed. Malcolm Cowley (New York: Charles Scribner's Sons, 1951), pp. 263–64.

20. "Financing Finnegan," *Esquire*, January, 1938; reprinted in *The Stories of F. Scott Fitzgerald*, p. 449.

21. "Emotional Bankruptcy," *Saturday Evening Post*, August 15, 1931.

22. *The Letters*, pp. 15–16.

23. *Ibid.*, p. 55.

24. "The Crack-Up," *Esquire*, February, 1936; reprinted in *The Crack-Up*, p. 71.

25. "Sleeping and Waking," *Esquire*, December, 1934; reprinted in *The Crack-Up*, p. 67.

26. *The Letters*, p. 36.

27. Wright Morris, "The Function of Nostalgia: F. Scott Fitzgerald," *The Territory Ahead* (New York: Harcourt, Brace & World, 1958); reprinted in *F. Scott Fitzgerald—A Collection of Critical Essays*, ed. Arthur Mizener (Englewood Cliffs, N. J.: Prentice Hall, 1963), p. 26.

28. "Echoes of the Jazz Age," *Scribner's Magazine*, November, 1931; reprinted in *The Crack-Up*, p. 22.

29. See *The Crack-Up*, p. 13. Fitzgerald connected the years 1919 to 1929 with the period of his own youth. On the night the stock market crashed, the Fitzgeralds were in Europe and stayed at the Beau Rivage in St. Raphael in the room Ring Lardner had occupied in 1924 (see "Show Mr. and Mrs. F. to Number—," *The Crack-Up*, p. 50). This is another one of the many coincidences in Fitzgerald's life because Lardner, whom he depicted in *Tender Is the Night*, was Fitzgerald's personification of deterioration and wasted genius; and that October night, on the eve of the depression, in Lardner's old room, Fitzgerald buried his youth.

30. Turnbull, p. 307.

31. *The Letters*, p. 578.

32. *Ibid.*, p. 32.

3—*This Side of Paradise*

1. *The Letters of F. Scott Fitzgerald*, ed. Andrew Turnbull (New York: Charles Scribner's Sons, 1963), p. 595.

2. F. Scott Fitzgerald, *This Side of Paradise* (New York: Charles Scribner's Sons, 1960), p. 194. All further quotations are from this edition, page reference indicated in brackets after the quote.

3. *The Apprentice Fiction of F. Scott Fitzgerald 1909–1917*, ed. John Kuehl (New Brunswick: Rutgers University Press, 1965). All quotations in this chapter from Fitzgerald's apprentice writing will be cited to this edition, page reference indicated in brackets after the quote.

4. Cf. Andrew Turnbull, *Scott Fitzgerald* (New York: Charles Scribner's Sons, 1962), p. 158.

5. In "The Crack-Up," Fitzgerald said: "my two juvenile regrets [were] not being big enough (or good enough) to play football in college, and not getting overseas during the war . . ." (*The Crack-Up*, p. 70; cf. also p. 84). When he died on December 21, 1940, Fitzgerald was reading *The Princeton Alumni Weekly*, making marginal notes about the Princeton football team.

6. Compton Mackenzie, *Sinister Street* (London: Macdonald & Co., 1949), p. 372. All further quotations are from this edition, page reference indicated in brackets after the quote.

7. Stephen Vincent Benét, *The Beginning of Wisdom* (New York: Henry Holt, 1921), p. 324.

8. Floyd Dell, *The Briary-Bush* (New York: Alfred A. Knopf, 1921), p. 369.

9. John Dos Passos, *Streets of Night* (New York: George H. Doran Co., 1923), p. 180.

10. *The Letters*, p. 462.

11. Edmund Wilson, "The Literary Spotlight; F. Scott Fitzgerald," *The Bookman*, LV (March, 1922), pp. 21–22.

12. James E. Miller, Jr., *The Fictional Technique of Scott Fitzgerald* (The Hague: Martinus Nijhoff, 1957), p. 26.

4—The Beautiful and Damned

1. Edmund Wilson, "The Literary Spotlight; F. Scott Fitzgerald," *The Bookman*, LV (March, 1922), p. 24.

2. *The Letters of F. Scott Fitzgerald*, ed. Andrew Turnbull (New York: Charles Scribner's Sons, 1963), p. 84.

3. F. Scott Fitzgerald, *The Beautiful and Damned* (New York: Charles Scribner's Sons, 1922), p. 41. All further quotations are from this edition, page reference indicated in brackets after the quote.

4. Andrew Turnbull, *Scott Fitzgerald* (New York: Charles Scribner's Sons, 1962), p. 131.

5. James E. Miller, Jr., *The Fictional Technique of Scott Fitzgerald* (The Hague: Martinus Nijhoff, 1957), p. 41.

6. H. L. Mencken, *Prejudices: Second Series* (New York: Alfred A. Knopf, 1920), p. 41.

7. Miller, p. 54.

8. *Ibid.*, p. 59.

9. Woodward Boyd, "The Fitzgerald Legend," *St. Paul Daily News*, December 10, 1922.

10. F. Scott Fitzgerald, *Tales of the Jazz Age* (New York: Charles Scribner's Sons, 1922), p. 93.

11. The whole canon of Fitzgerald's fiction shows the influence of Keats. The title *Tender Is the Night* comes from a line in "Ode to a Nightingale," and Fitzgerald had once intended to title his second novel *The Beautiful Lady Without Mercy*, after Keats's "La Belle Dame sans Merci," before he finally decided on the title *The Beautiful and Damned* (see *The Letters*, pp. 464–65).

12. Fitzgerald's preoccupation with deterioration and physical decline was probably influenced by his reading of Harold Frederic's *The Damnation of Theron Ware* and Frank Norris' *Vandover and the Brute*. In a letter to Sinclair Lewis, written at the time that he was working on *The Beautiful and Damned*, Fitzgerald wrote: "I want to tell you that *Main Street* has displaced *Thereon Ware* in my favor as the best American novel" (*The Letters*, p. 467). Fitzgerald wrote Maxwell Perkins on February 3, 1920 that he "just discovered" Frank Norris. "I think *McTeague* and *Vandover* are both excellent" (*The Letters*, p. 144). And in a letter to James Branch Cabell, dated Christmas 1920, Fitzgerald wrote: "I have just finished an extraordinary novel called *The Beautiful Lady Without Mercy* which shows touches of your influence, much of Mencken, and not a little of Frank Norris" (*The Letters*, p. 464).

5—The Great Gatsby

1. *The Letters, of F. Scott Fitzgerald*, ed. Andrew Turnbull (New York: Charles Scribner's Sons, 1963), p. 173.

2. "A Woman with a Past," *Saturday Evening Post*, September 6, 1930; reprinted in *Taps at Reveille* (New York: Charles Scribner's Sons, 1935), p. 193. All further quotations from this story will be cited to this edition, page reference indicated in brackets after the quote.

3. Fitzgerald's Ledger, p. 70. The total context of these quotes as they appear in the Ledger are as follows: "Aug 1916 —Lake Forest. Peg Carry. Petting Party. Ginevra. Party. The bad day at the McCormicks. The dinner at Pegs. Disapointment. Mary Birlard Pierce. Little Marjorie King [Ginevra's sister] & her smile. Beautiful Billy Mitchell [whom Ginevra eventually married]. Peg Carry stands straight. " 'Poor boys

shouldn't think of marrying rich girls." Aunt Millie forced Belgium kids to sing Die watch am Rhine.' "

4. Mrs. Marjorie King Belden, Ginevra's sister, told me (February 21, 1965) that there were abrasive feelings between Fitzgerald and Charles King.

5. "Winter Dreams," *Metropolitan Magazine*, December, 1922; reprinted in *All the Sad Young Men* (New York: Charles Scribner's Sons, 1926), p. 90. All further quotations from this story will be cited to this edition, page reference indicated in brackets after the quote.

6. Andrew Turnbull, *Scott Fitzgerald* (New York: Charles Scribner's Sons, 1962), p. 150.

7. "Show Mr. and Mrs. F. to Number—," *Esquire*, May–June, 1934; reprinted in *The Crack-Up*, p. 50.

8. *The Letters*, p. 19. This experience later became the basis for the story "Three Hours Between Planes," published in *Esquire*, July of 1941, and reprinted in *The Stories of F. Scott Fitzgerald*, pp. 464–69.

9. *The Letters*, p. 173.

10. George Jean Nathan, "Memories of Fitzgerald, Lewis, and Dreiser," *Esquire*, L (October, 1958), p. 149.

11. Edmund Wilson, *This Room and This Gin and These Sandwiches* (New York: *The New Republic*, 1937), pp. 75–76.

12. *New York Times*, November 14, 1922, p. 31:2.

13. Arthur Garfield Hays, *City Lawyer* (New York: Simon and Schuster, 1942).

14. *The Letters*, p. 551.

15. *Ibid.*, p. 358.

16. F. Scott Fitzgerald, *The Great Gatsby* (New York: Charles Scribner's Sons, 1953), p. 83. All further quotations are from this edition, page reference indicated in brackets after the quote.

17. *The Apprentice Fiction of F. Scott Fitzgerald 1909–1917*, ed. John Kuehl (New Brunswick: Rutgers University Press, 1965), p. 170. All further quotations from this story will be cited to this edition, page reference indicated in brackets after the quote. John Kuehl has discussed the theme of unrequited love in this story and *The Great Gatsby* and compared George Rombert to Tom Buchanan. Cf. "A Note on the Begetting of Gatsby," *University: A Princeton Magazine*, No. 21 (Summer, 1964), pp. 26–32.

18. " 'O Russet Witch,' " *Metropolitan Magazine*, February, 1921; reprinted in *Tales of the Jazz Age*, p. 254.

19. "The Diamond as Big as the Ritz," *Smart Set*, June 1922; reprinted in *Tales of the Jazz Age*, p. 191.

20. "The Sensible Thing," *Liberty*, July 5, 1924; reprinted in *All the Sad Young Men*, p. 219. All further quotations from this story will be cited to this edition, page reference indicated in brackets after the quote.

21. "Absolution," *American Mercury*, June, 1924; reprinted in *All the Sad Young Men*, p. 130. All further quotations from this story will be cited to this edition, page reference indicated in brackets after the quote.

22. There is more than one suggestion that Gatsby is a kind of sacrificial priest. When Nick first sees him, Gatsby, like a priest on the altar, "stretched out his arms toward the dark water [toward, that is, the green light on Daisy's dock]" [21]. Nick also observes Gatsby under "a wafer of a moon" [56], and talks about Gatsby committing "himself to the following of a grail" [149]. When Nick observes Gatsby standing watch over Daisy's house, Gatsby turned away, "as though [Nick's] presence marred the sacredness of the vigil" [146]. There are religious overtones throughout the novel. When Myrtle Wilson dies, for example, she "*knelt* in the road and mingled her thick dark blood with the dust" [138, italics mine]. Since Myrtle was killed instantly, Fitzgerald is using the word "knelt" in a way to suggest that Myrtle's death is part of the religious pattern of the novel.

23. For a further discussion of this point see Thomas Hanzo's "The Theme and Narrator of *The Great Gatsby*," *Modern Fiction Studies*, II (Winter, 1956–57), 183–90.

24. *The Crack-Up*, ed. Edmund Wilson (New York: New Directions, 1956), p. 69.

25. *The Letters*, p. 173.

26. *The Letters*, p. 341; for the letter to Mencken see p. 480.

27. Arthur Mizener, *The Far Side of Paradise* (Boston: Houghton Mifflin, 1951), p. 171.

28. John Henry Raleigh, "F. Scott Fitzgerald's *The Great Gatsby*: Legendary Bases and Allegorical Significance," *The University of Kansas City Review*, XXIV (Autumn, 1957); reprinted in Mizener's *A Collection of Critical Essays*, p. 101.

29. Marius Bewley, *The Eccentric Design, Form in the Classic American Novel* (New York: Columbia University Press, 1959), p. 265.

30. *Ibid.*, p. 284.

31. Edwin Fussell, "Fitzgerald's Brave New World," *ELH*, XIX (December, 1952); reprinted in Mizener's *A Collection of Critical Essays*, p. 44.

32. "Early Success," *The Crack-Up*, p. 89.

33. *Ibid.*, p. 90.

34. Fussell, p. 43.

35. Reference to the frontier runs through the novel. The novel opens with mention of Columbus: East Egg and West Egg are like Columbus' eggs. Dan Cody is depicted as the last of the frontiersmen. And Nick says, "I was a guide, a pathfinder, an original settler" [4].

36. For the view that Eckleburg is a symbol of Fitzgerald's belief in a benevolent God, see Milton Hindus, "The Eyes of T. J. Eckleburg," *Boston University Studies in English*, III (Spring, 1957), 22–31. I see nothing in the resolution of the novel that supports this view.

37. Besides the accident involving the owl-eyed man (54–56), Nick tells Jordan Baker, " 'You're a rotten driver. . . . Either you ought to be more careful, or you oughtn't to drive at all' " [59]. Tom Buchanan gets into an accident outside of Santa Barbara, California, and the chambermaid who was with him broke her arm [78].

6—Tender Is the Night

1. Calvin Tomkins, "Living Well Is the Best Revenge," *New Yorker*, XXXVIII (July 28, 1962), pp. 43–44.

2. *Ibid.*, p. 31.

3. Morley Callaghan, *That Summer in Paris* (New York: Coward-McCann, 1963), p. 191.

4. *The Letters of F. Scott Fitzgerald*, ed. Andrew Turnbull (New York: Charles Scribner's Sons, 1963), p. 230.

5. F. Scott Fitzgerald, *Tender Is the Night* (New York: Charles Scribner's Sons, 1934), p. 200. All further quotations are from this edition, page reference indicated in brackets after the quote.

6. George Jean Nathan, "Memories of Fitzgerald, Lewis and Dreiser," *Esquire*, L (October, 1958), pp. 148–49.

7. See Matthew J. Bruccoli, *The Composition of Tender Is*

the Night (Pittsburgh: University of Pittsburgh Press, 1963), p. 18. Bruccoli's book is a thorough and useful study of Fitzgerald's seventeen drafts of the novel.

8. Calvin Tomkins, *New Yorker*, p. 50.

9. "The World's Fair," *Kenyon Review*, X (Autumn, 1948), pp. 567–78.

10. *The Letters*, p. 19.

11. "A Nice Quiet Place" was originally published in the *Saturday Evening Post*, May 31, 1930.

12. F. Scott Fitzgerald, *Taps at Reveille*, (New York: Charles Scribner's Sons, 1935), p. 169.

13. *The Letters*, p. 79.

14. *Ibid.*, p. 32.

15. *Ibid.*, p. 346.

16. Andrew Turnbull, *Scott Fitzgerald* (New York: Charles Scribner's Sons, 1962), p. 150.

17. *The Crack-Up*, ed. Edmund Wilson (New York: New Directions, 1956), p. 180.

18. *Ibid.*, p. 209.

19. Turnbull, p. 261.

20. "Handle with Care," *Esquire*, March, 1936; reprinted in *The Crack-Up*, p. 77.

21. Turnbull, p. 265.

22. "The Crack-Up" and "Handle with Care," *The Crack-Up*, pp. 71 and 77.

23. *The Letters*, pp. 289–90.

24. Mosby (Fitzgerald misspelled the name "Moseby"), born in 1833 and died in 1916, organized a group of rangers which became Company A, 43rd Battalion Partisan Rangers of the Confederate army. This band created havoc with the Union troops fighting in northern Virginia. Mosby's most famous exploits were kidnapping General Stoughton out of his own headquarters on May 9, 1863; raiding Points of Rock, Maryland, on July 4, 1864; and seizing $168,000 from Union troops on October 14, 1864.

25. *The Apprentice Fiction of F. Scott Fitzgerald 1909–1917*, ed. John Kuehl (New Brunswick: Rutgers University Press, 1965), p. 67.

26. "The Last of the Belles," *Saturday Evening Post*, March 2, 1929; reprinted in *Taps at Reveille*, p. 258. All further quotations from this story will be cited to this edition, page reference indicated in brackets after the quote.

27. "The Rich Boy," *Redbook*, January–February, 1926; reprinted in *All the Sad Young Men*, p. 56.

28. "Two Wrongs," *Saturday Evening Post*, January 18, 1930; reprinted in *Taps at Reveille*, p. 242. All further quotations from this story will be cited to this edition, page reference indicated in brackets after the quote.

29. "One Trip Abroad," *Saturday Evening Post*, October 11, 1930; reprinted in *Afternoon of an Author*, ed. Arthur Mizener (Princeton, N. J.: Princeton University Library, 1957), p. 165.

30. "The Rough Crossing," *Saturday Evening Post*, June 8, 1929; reprinted in *The Short Stories of F. Scott Fitzgerald*, ed. Malcolm Cowley (New York: Charles Scribner's Sons, 1951), pp. 263–64. All further quotations from this story will be cited to this edition, page reference indicated in brackets after the quote.

31. "Babylon Revisited," *Saturday Evening Post*, February 21, 1931; reprinted in *Taps at Reveille*, p. 384. All further quotations from this story will be cited to this edition, page reference indicated in brackets after the quote.

32. Wayne C. Booth, *The Rhetoric of Fiction* (Chicago: University of Chicago Press, 1961), pp. 192–95.

7—Count of Darkness, The Last Tycoon, and The Pat Hobby Stories

1. *The Letters of F. Scott Fitzgerald*, ed. Andrew Turnbull (New York: Charles Scribner's Sons, 1963), p. 263.

2. *Ibid.*, p. 283.

3. F. Scott Fitzgerald, "In the Darkest Hour," *Redbook*, October, 1934, p. 16.

4. *Ibid.*, p. 18.

5. F. Scott Fitzgerald, "Gods of Darkness," *Redbook*, November, 1941, p. 81.

6. Hitler, of course, did not open his Russian Campaign until June 22, 1941, six months after Fitzgerald's death. The split between Germany and Russia was growing, however, in 1940, and the final break came in November of 1940 when Germany refused the Russian's counterproposals on the Balkans' problem. Before the end of that year, Hitler had ordered operation "Barbarossa," his plan of attack against Russia. A great many people had felt, even after Russia had signed a nonagression treaty with the Nazis on August 22,

1939, that hope depended on Russia eventually entering the war against Germany, hence forcing her to fight on two fronts. If Part Fourt of *Count of Darkness* is as allegorical as it seems, Fitzgerald must have had something like this in mind.

7. F. Scott Fitzgerald, *The Last Tycoon, An Unfinished Novel* (Charles Scribner's Sons, 1941), p. 135. All further quotations are from this edition, page reference indicated in brackets after the quote.

8. *The Letters*, p. 32.

9. See Andrew Turnbull, *Scott Fitzgerald* (New York: Charles Scribner's Sons, 1962), p. 202.

10. *The Letters*, p. 564.

11. Sheilah Graham and Gerold Frank, *Beloved Infidel* (New York: Bantam Books, 1959), p. 243.

12. This theme can be found elsewhere in *The Last Tycoon*, although the tone is playful. Speaking of John Broaca, the director, who worked into each of his movies a scene showing a girl surrounded by dogs and then slapping "a horse on the rump," Fitzgerald says, with tongue in cheek, "the explanation was probably Freudian; more likely that at a drab moment in youth he had looked through a fence and seen a beautiful girl with dogs and horses. As a trademark for glamor it was stamped on his brain forever" [37]. Despite his jocularity, Fitzgerald believed, as we have seen in *The Great Gatsby*, that one all too easily can be arrested by what he finds glamorous in his youth. Fitzgerald, by the way, considered Broaca a has-been "at thirty."

13. F. Scott Fitzgerald, *The Pat Hobby Stories* (New York: Charles Scribner's Sons, 1962). All quotations are from this edition, page reference indicated in brackets after the quote.

14. John Aldridge, "Fitzgerald: The Horror and the Vision of Paradise," *After the Lost Generation* (New York: McGraw-Hill, 1951); reprinted in Mizener's *A Collection of Critical Essays*, p. 42.

8—The Limits of Vision

1. Isidor Schneider, "A Pattern of Failure," *New Masses*, LVII (December 4, 1945), 23–24.

2. John Berryman, "F. Scott Fitzgerald," *Kenyon Review*, VIII (Winter, 1946), 103–12.

3. Ernest Hemingway, *A Moveable Feast* (New York: Charles Scribner's Sons, 1964), p. 155.

4. Fitzgerald replied to Mencken's charge that *The Great Gatsby* is trivial. Cf. *The Letters*, p. 480.

5. Edward Dahlberg, "The Fitzgerald Revival: A Dissent," *Freeman*, II (November 5, 1951), 90–92.

6. Henry Dan Piper, *F. Scott Fitzgerald: A Critical Portrait* (New York: Holt, Rinehart and Winston, 1965), p. 107.

7. *Ibid.*, p. 111.

8. In this connection, it is interesting that Jordan Baker's aunt is named Sigourney.

9. *The Letters of F. Scott Fitzgerald*, ed. Andrew Turnbull (New York: Charles Scribner's Sons, 1963), p. 191.

10. *Ibid.*, p. 399.

BIBLIOGRAPHY

I. PRIMARY SOURCES

The Apprentice Fiction of F. Scott Fitzgerald—1909–1917, ed. John Kuehl. New Brunswick: Rutgers University Press, 1965.

This Side of Paradise. New York: Charles Scribner's Sons, 1920.

Flappers and Philosophers. New York: Charles Scribner's Sons, 1921.

The Beautiful and Damned. New York: Charles Scribner's Sons, 1922.

Tales of the Jazz Age. New York: Charles Scribner's Sons, 1922.

The Great Gatsby. New York: Charles Scribner's Sons, 1925.

All the Sad Young Men. New York: Charles Scribner's Sons, 1926.

Tender Is the Night. New York: Charles Scribner's Sons, 1934.

Taps at Reveille. New York: Charles Scribner's Sons, 1935.

Count of Darkness. Redbook: I. "In the Dark Hour," October, 1934; II. "The Count of Darkness," June, 1935; III. "A Kingdom in the Dark," August, 1935; IV. "Gods of Darkness," November, 1941.

The Last Tycoon, ed. Edmund Wilson. New York: Charles Scribner's Sons, 1941.

The Crack-Up, ed. Edmund Wilson. New York: New Directions, 1945.

The Stories of F. Scott Fitzgerald, intro. Malcolm Cowley. New York: Charles Scribner's Sons, 1951.

Afternoon of an Author; A Selection of Uncollected Stories and Essays, intro. and notes Arthur Mizener. Princeton, N. J.: Princeton University Library, 1957.

The Pat Hobby Stories, ed. Arnold Gingrich. New York: Charles Scribner's Sons, 1962.

The Letters of F. Scott Fitzgerald, ed. and intro. Andrew Turnbull. New York: Charles Scribner's Sons, 1963.

II. CHECK LISTS

Mizener, Arthur, "Fitzgerald's Published Work," *The Far Side of Paradise.* Boston: Houghton Mifflin, 1951.

Piper, Henry Dan, "F. Scott Fitzgerald: A Check List." *Princeton University Library Chronicle,* XII (Summer, 1951), 196–208.

Porter, Bernard H., "The First Publications of F. Scott Fitzgerald." *Twentieth Century Literature,* V (January, 1960), 176–82.

Beebe, Maurice and Jackson R. Bryer, "Criticism of F. Scott Fitzgerald: A Selected Checklist." *Modern Fiction Studies,* VII (Spring, 1961), 82–94.

Bryer, Jackson R., "F. Scott Fitzgerald and His Critics: A Bibliographical Record." *Bulletin of Bibliography,* XXIII (1962), 155–58, 180–83, 201–8.

Bryer, Jackson R., "F. Scott Fitzgerald: A Review of Research and Scholarship." *Texas Studies in Literature and Language,* V (Spring, 1963), 147–63.

III. BIOGRAPHIES

Mizener, Arthur, *The Far Side of Paradise.* Boston: Houghton Mifflin, 1951; reprinted in a Vintage paperback.

Graham, Sheilah and Gerold Frank, *Beloved Infidel.* New York: Henry Holt, 1958; reprinted by Bantam Books.

Turnbull, Andrew, *Scott Fitzgerald.* New York: Charles Scribner's Sons, 1962.

IV. CRITICAL AND TEXTUAL BOOKS

Miller, James E., Jr., *The Fictional Technique of Scott Fitzgerald.* The Hague: Martinus Nijhoff, 1957.

Perosa, Sergio, *L'Arte di F. Scott Fitzgerald.* Rome: Edizioni di Storia e Letteratura, 1961.

Shain, Charles E., *F. Scott Fitzgerald.* Minneapolis: University of Minnesota Pamphlets on America Writers, 1961.

Eble, Kenneth, *F. Scott Fitzgerald.* New York: Twayne Publishers, 1963.

Bruccoli, Matthew J., *The Composition of Tender Is the Night: A Study of the Manuscripts.* Pittsburgh: University of Pittsburgh Press, 1963.

Goldhurst, William, *F. Scott Fitzgerald and his Con-*

temporaries. New York: The World Publishing Co., 1963.
Piper, Henry Dan, *F. Scott Fitzgerald: A Critical Portrait*. New York: Holt, Rinehart and Winston, Inc., 1965.

v. CRITICAL COLLECTIONS

Kazin, Alfred, *F. Scott Fitzgerald: The Man and His Work*. Cleveland: World Publishing Co., 1951; reprinted in paperback by Collier Books.
Hoffman, Frederick J., *The Great Gatsby: A Study*. New York: Charles Scribner's Sons, 1962.
Mizener, Arthur, *F. Scott Fitzgerald: A Collection of Critical Essays*. Englewood, N. J.: Prentice-Hall, 1963.

INDEX